SHAT
THE MYTHS

© 1992

'LARGE ACCOMPLISHMENTS ARE
THE RESULTS OF SMALL GAINS'

BY

DAVID L. BROWN

Copyright © 1995 by David L. Brown

All rights reserved.
No part of this book may be reproduced or
utilized in any form or by any means, electronic
or mechanical, including photocopying,
recording or by any information storage and
retrieval system, without permission in writing
from the Publisher. Inquiries should be
addressed to:

If Productions
P. O. Box 11485
Killeen, Texas 76547-1148
(817) 539-8064

Library of Congress
Catalog-in-Publication Number 95-78466

ISBN Number 0-9647906-0-2

Printed in the United States of America
at Morgan Printing in Austin, Texas

Dedicated to
my wife
who's as much an inspiration to me
as the leaf-bearing dove was to Noah

CONTENTS

ACKNOWLEDGMENTS

I gratefully acknowledge the three people whose unexplainable assistance helped bring this five-year endeavor to fruition. My wife Barbara the artist, my editor, Mr. Luther C. Powell, and co-editor Ms. Donna J. Mills-Curry. And a great big thanks to the staff of Panama Medical Services, Inc. Without them the Myths could not have been Shattered.

FORWARD

No American born citizen needs to think that the natural process of BIRTH is a CURSE! We do not choose our cultures, we belong to them. In spite of the efforts of our forefathers to ensure equal birthright privileges to all American born citizens, for the most part, their efforts appear to have been in vain. Unfortunately for numerous Blacks and citizens of color their culture indicates entrapment that often results in both misunderstanding and imprisonment. Stated simply; the topic is cultural differences but it hardly describes the nature of discussion.

Regarding the nation's image dilemma in the areas of social and economics, Blacks are seen as both the cause and the solution. Such teachings are designed to destroy the morale of American citizens and corrupt national unity. Furthermore such ideology does not have merit whenever a thorough examination into America's policy of fair play (founding policies) is conducted. For decades Blacks were not allowed to even attempt to learn the principles of reading, writing, and arithmetic. Obviously during this time period in America's history, Blacks lost valuable study time and development of study tactics that must be attributed to why Blacks experience the difficulties that they do when taking the "SAT" and other similar tests.

Historians have documented Blacks' plight on the employment front during such time period as dismal to say the least. There is also the probability that during this moment in America's history that perhaps the curse of race blemished the nation's cultural picture. In all likelihood during this scenario Affirmative Action, The Voting Rights Act and other such laws were destined to become national requirements.

There happens to be an avalanche of bleak scenarios unfolding throughout numerous Black communities across America. It suggests to this nation's Blacks in a harsh tone saying: "you're unable to change reality and powerless to change your status". If such be the case; perhaps the U.S. Constitution with its constructive elements misled us. Needless to say a suggestion to help cure whatever ails us, so that it will not afflict those coming up behind us, but instead positively affect them, must be agreed upon.

Even though there is a narrow window of opportunity for total acknowledgment for all of the contributions made by American born Blacks, there are some men and women who's contributions can not be ignored. Due in part to these noteworthy Black pioneers lay the answers to many of the dilemmas that confront present day Blacks.

There is an old Chinese proverb that says, "he who is afraid of asking is ashamed of learning". Therefore, I ask Black Americans, "why not challenge our offspring to develop some of our noted role models similar traits, by doing so, they may display some of their inherited characteristics?" Truth is young people often grow up to be exactly what they hear early in their lives that they can or will be. That's why it is so important for them to get the right message early. If young Black boys are told they can grow up to be just like Mr. Booker T. Washington, Honorable Thurgood Marshall, or Dr. Martin Luther

King Jr. they will develop a positive attitude. Dr. King and the likes wrestled freedom from the nation for the descendants of the nation's slaves. Therefore in regards to role models no one should underestimate the seriousness of its long term effects.

It is both sad and unfortunate that the winds of change have not blown the sediments of prejudice from America's grass roots. An even greater disturbing perception indicates that the attitude of the courts mirrors that of the country. Such a paradox is evident in the relationship between the nation's two largest groups—Black and White Americans. However, the grievances between Blacks and white seem to create such an unsettling void that no mortal man nor group of mortal men are likely to fill it. Stated simply the nation's citizens need to witness another (Immaculate Conception) miracle.

There is little doubt that many Americans live in a state of quiet desperation because along with the title of US citizen many Americans shoulder an even greater responsibility—that of contributor. The land of the free and the home of the brave is also the land where, "Affection is the soil that contains the roots of wholesome existence." Within every previously noted instance lies an unseen obstacle called survival. In order to survive in this country one must have a means to generate money. Money is the ultimate ingredient required to convert dreams to reality. Without a doubt this nation's cultural differences exist because of the desire to have reality reflect one's dreams.

Needless to say, today America is faced with the urgency of the moment. Today's chaos could very well be tomorrow's norm in disguise. Normalcy for the second largest group of American citizens is triggered by tragedy. The tragic characterization of Black role models and the Black population as a whole is unfair and untrue. However, as global discontent grows regarding America and its citizens, there is no time for any one to practice malice because every able-bodied citizen is needed in order for this nation to retain its status as the world's leader. A blueprint detailing change for such a task isn't easy to devise. However, the ideology expressed throughout *Shattering The Myths* and similar formulas like, "Large achievements are the results of small gains," are capable of producing solutions to our national dilemma.

From time to time it has been said that America is the world's melting pot. The concept of *Shattering The Myths* appeals to the nation's conscious to stir the contents of her pot.

1 *HYPNOTIC DISCOVERY*

EXTRA! EXTRA! Read all about it as, America's Blacks discover that in regards to assumptions everything old is new again!" Recognition that comes by way of handles and titles is associated with power. Therefore the title African American leader has a status of little meaning. The toilsome thing about being a Black leader lies in the term itself. Stated simply, his efforts go unnoticed, and his presence usually equates to nothing more than a mere silhouette. Citizens of a country where it is said anyone can become president, Blacks can be excused for desiring to become mayors. Their excuse lies within the interpretation of such eloquent phrases as "We hold these truths to be self-evident, that all men are created equal." On the other hand their remedies lie within such phrases as "IN

1

GOD WE TRUST" which enable them to shatter numerous myths that corrupt and distort potential.

Documentation by various historians indicate that even before the first landings American soil has been populated with multiethnic groups. The passage of time has produced enormous strife among this nation's citizens. However, none is more pronounced than the perplexing dilemma that exists between Blacks and Whites. Even though co-existence produced both measurable and memorable experiences, the United States has reverted back to the sectionalism that threatened our nation over 100 years ago. To separate ourselves into a black America and a white America is dangerous. It scares me to think that somewhere over the years we've missed the boat.

Regardless of its problems, America remains the best country on earth. Therefore tourists flock to visit by the millions annually. Harlem is not the New York most tourist come to see—the prestige once associated with this part of the city no longer exists. Instead Harlem has been transformed from a once thriving Black business district and cultural mecca to a crime and drug infested "utopia." Nonetheless, Harlem is home to many law abiding Black citizens and other minorities, who at various times require the assistance of the police, firefighter, and paramedics in securing and preserving their well-being. These and other public safety officials provide their professional service to other residents of the city but with a much greater sense of urgency.

On this balmy October day in Harlem, at 135th street and Malcolm "X" Boulevard where the Thompson family live, Thelma is in the too familiar process of changing her one-year-old daughter's pamper when she discovers that her usual stack of 10 to 12 pampers that she keeps in the kitchen are gone. She calls out to her youngest son L.T., "Bring mama a pamper from the closet in the living room." L.T., who is 8 years old, is lying belly down on the uncarpeted living room floor watching the evening news.

Why, you ask yourself, is an eight-year-old ghetto boy watching the evening news? Simply because channel 17 is the clearest channel on their T.V. that has no cable and is at least twice as old as he is. Hearing his mother's request, L.T. answers, "Yes ma'am" then quickly jumps up and gets a diaper and proudly carries it to his mother. Thelma takes the pamper from her son, smiles and gives him an approving wink of the eye and then says "Thank you sweetheart. I don't know what I'd do without you." She then finishes her task at hand. Sensing that she is getting a little tired due to the fact that she's eight months pregnant, Thelma lays Pamela into the playpen located near the kitchen window. Afterwards she waddles over to the refrigerator and starts to sift through for something to cook for dinner. While browsing through the contents in the refrigerator, Thelma begins to feel light-headed and falls to the floor before she can sit down in a chair only a few feet away. Having heard a loud thump from the kitchen area, L.T. immediately runs into the kitchen where he finds his mother lying on the floor, unconscious. His eyes become diluted in apprehension and his little heart pumps hard! Overcome by fear and anxiety, L.T. kneels down and grabs a hold of Thelma's left hand then calls out to her pleadingly, "Mama, mama it's me L.T. Say something." She doesn't answer. Then he takes his right index and thumb fingers and gently lifts up her left eyelid. Thelma's eyes are dilated. While simultaneously scanning her body, L.T. suddenly discovers that the right side of his mother's pink maternity dress is covered with blood!

His adrenaline is now running wild! But in a sudden rush of calmness, L.T. remembers his 3rd grade class field trip to the fire station and what the fire marshal said about calling 911 in case of an emergency. He recalls that you must tell the 911 operator your name, address and the problem, and whether you need a fireman, ambulance or policeman. So, without hesitation L.T. runs to the phone and dials 911. "Hello. May I help you?" the operator asks.

"Hello, my name is L.T. and my address is 207 East 135th street and Malcolm X Boulevard my apartment number is 15! It's my Mama, she is bleeding and I can't wake her up," L.T. says in a fast but low tone of voice.

The operator asks, "Is this a kid? Honey, you'll have to speak louder I can hardly hear you." She adds, "Please don't play on this line. It is for emergencies only," and hangs up!

Determination and fear for his mother's life forces L.T. to dial 911 again. This time he repeats himself but in a much louder and clearer tone. The same operator receives his call and she knows that this is not a prank. Immediately three things rush through her mind: she knows this is a child and that his mother is unconscious and bleeding; she knows that an ambulance will more than likely not respond to that address; and just as important she knows that she can't inform this child of such a cruel possibility. So instead of enlightening the child with the problems of a melting-pot democracy, the operator calmly instructs L.T., "Put some ice in a washcloth and hold it firmly against your mother's forehead until she awakes, or an ambulance arrives. Now, L.T. whatever you do don't hang up the phone!" she exclaimed.

Upon hearing the operator's instructions L.T. drops the receiver and runs into the bathroom where he grabs his washcloth then dashes back into the kitchen. The freezer compartment of the refrigerator nearly flies off its hinges as L.T. grabs a tray of ice. He put four cubes into his washcloth. He pushes the freezer shut, grabs a hold of the receiver, and then sits down on the floor where he places Thelma's head across his lap and gently lays the ice-filled washcloth against her forehead. Meanwhile, the operator yells for L.T. to say something, at which time L.T. replies, "I'm back." The operator breathes a sigh of relief. The minutes seem to last hours. Actually only about three minutes pass before Thelma slowly begins to regain consciousness. L.T. quickly releases the phone which at times seems as if it is an extension of his ear. "Mama, mama are you alright?" he asks anxiously. Thelma only manages to utter a groaning sound. Suddenly, L.T. hears someone enter the front door. He thinks perhaps it is the paramedics; instead it's his father. Albert is a big man— he stands 6'4" and weighs approximately 240 pounds. At one time he played football at Syracuse, however due to a knee injury he only completed two years. Albert has a habit of going into the kitchen first because that's usually where he finds his high school sweetheart. "Help! help! I'm in the kitchen," L.T. shouts. Hearing L.T.'s call Albert races into the kitchen where he discovers semiconscious Thelma and L.T. in a pool of blood and Pamela in her playpen crying at the top of her lungs! Meanwhile, a concerned operator is yelling over the phone. Sweat begins to literally pour from his forehead, Albert's mouth feels as dry as cotton, and everybody's dilemma is adding stress to this crisis. Albert quickly pulls himself together and kneels down to check on Thelma. "Honey, it's okay now. I'm here," he softly assures her. Albert assesses the situation while listening to L.T. He knows that he must get Thelma to the hospital fast. Even though her eyes are still closed Thelma whispers to Albert, "Give Pamela her bottle from the refrigerator." He promptly replies "Okay, honey." While getting the baby's bottle, Albert orders L.T. to run next door and get Shirley. L.T. carefully lifts Thelma's head from his lap, then jumps up and runs next door. On his way to Pamela's playpen Albert picks up the receiver and identifies himself. The operator does too and informs him of all the details. The operator concludes by wishing the entire family good luck. Albert thanks her then hangs up. Afterwards he kneels down to comfort and inform Thelma saying, "Honey, it'll be alright. Hang in there. I'll get you to the hospital ASAP." Albert then lifts Thelma as gently as possible and heads for the front door. Before he gets to the door Shirley has it open. While holding L.T.'s hand they stand off to the side so the Thompsons could pass. Once

outside while continuing towards the car Albert asks
Shirley over his right shoulder, "Would you please keep
an eye on L.T. and Pamela while I drive Thelma to the
hospital?" Shirley assures him that she'll take care of
everything. At that moment L.T. snatches away from
Shirley, runs and opens the passenger's front door, then
jumps into the backseat. Albert's mind is on getting
Thelma to the hospital and he doesn't say a word as he
closes the door and darts around to the driver's side. Traffic
is uncommonly light considering the time (5:45 p.m.) of
day. Upon arrival at Harlem Hospital, Albert is practically
out of the car before he's parked. Quickly he runs around
and opens the passenger's door where he gently lifts
Thelma out and races to the emergency room. L.T. slams
the doors and hurries behind his parents. Once through
the sliding glass door, a nurse sees Albert carrying Thelma
and gets a wheelchair to assist. While placing Thelma into
the wheelchair, Albert emotionally briefs the nurse on the
previous chain of events. The R.N. immediately starts
yelling commands to the staff, "Get some vital signs on
her, she's eight months pregnant. I need 8cc of Demerol,
call obstetrics and have them set up for surgery. Give her
oxygen now!"

Meanwhile, Albert and L.T. stop at the admission desk
and complete insurance forms and other necessary paper-
work. Afterwards the nurse informs Albert that Thelma
has been taken to the obstetrics intensive care ward located on the 7th floor. Albert and L.T. sprint to the nearest elevator which is located at the end of the hall. In their
haste to get to the elevator they accidently knock over a
gurney but keep on sprinting to the elevator.

Finally they arrive at the 7th floor and again they
sprint from the elevator to the nurse's desk but this time
they don't knock over a gurney. The nurse at the desk asks
Albert, "May I help you sir?"

"Yes, they brought my wife up for delivery" he replies.
Continuing he asks, "I need to know how she's doing."

"What is the patient's name that you two have come to visit?" the nurse asks.

It's my mama, Mrs. Thelma Thompson," L.T. shouts. Unable to hold her smile, nonetheless she cuts it short then informs them that patient Thompson is in with Dr. Albright who's head of the Obstetric Department.

She adds, "You gentlemen will have to wait in the waiting room which is located down the hall, the last door on your left until further notice." The nurse could not help but notice the worrisome look on Albert's face. In an effort to ease his mind she says, "Mr. Thompson, please try not to worry. Dr. Albright is the best obstetrician in New York." Albert's expression doesn't change once inside the waiting room. As Albert and L.T. wait, the minutes seem as if they were hours. Albert, who's sitting on the edge of his chair, suddenly buries his head into his huge clasped hands for a moment, then begins shaking his hands uncontrollably as he stares aimlessly at the checkered floor. L.T. is sitting in the chair next to his father looking around the room in a childlike manner, his eyes roaming in search of something, yet nothing at all.

Meanwhile, in the delivery room Dr. Albright and his staff are working frantically to save both Thelma and her son. Thelma's blood pressure drops to 50/20 and suddenly her heart stops! Dr. Albright, surprised by these turn of events, doesn't panic but instead starts barking orders to his surgical team. "I need the heart fibrillator, give her 10cc of demerol, turn up the oxygen mask!" The staff reacts like a well-greased machine smoothly adhering to the doctor's orders. "Stand clear," shouts Dr. Albright as he prepares the electric shock pads on the fibrillator. He then rips open the hospital gown that Thelma is wearing, places the pads onto her chest, and presses the button that sends an electrical current through the pads and into Thelma's chest. The current hits her with such a force it lifts Thelma's entire body off the table! Her heart rate monitor still reads a flatline. Again Dr. Albright shouts, "Stand clear," as he prepares to give Thelma another jolt. Again the pads are positioned on Thelma's chest when suddenly the cardiologist shouts, "We have a heartbeat!" Throughout the delivery room a sigh of relief is felt by the staff.

Meanwhile, daylight no longer enters any of the huge waiting room windows. At this time numerous long tube shaped fluorescent lights light up the off-white walls which are accented with black leather and chrome furniture that rest upon a highly polished black and white checkered floor. The room's only occupants are L.T. and Albert. A fidgety L.T. climbs down from his chair and forces himself between his father's clasped hands and into his father's arms, then begins to question his father nonstop about his mother's condition, asking, "Daddy how much longer?"

"I don't know son," replies Albert.

Again L.T. questions, "Daddy do you think that because the ambulance didn't come will mean Mama have to stay here overnight?"

Again Albert answers, "Son I don't know that yet." Albert senses that L.T. is not about to stop questioning him anytime soon and therefore quickly takes charge of their conversation. Albert starts by praising L.T. stating, "You know son, your calling 911 was a very smart and grown-up thing to do." He adds, "It is that kind of action that sometimes make me think that you might have a mystical link to the men whom you are named after." Now that comment grabs L.T.'s attention like nothing else before. Albert then asks L.T., "What do your initials stand for?"

L.T. responds by shouting, "My name is Luther Taliaferro Thompson!" Immediately following L.T.'s ear-piercing reply, the waiting room door swings open and Dr. Albright appears. He motions for Albert to come to him. As he walks toward the doctor Albert tries to read the doctor's facial expression but cannot. Dr. Albright introduces himself then proceeds right away to explain the dilemma that he and his staff face in the operating room, including what decision Albert might have to make. The doctor informs Albert that a caesarean section must be performed due to the amount of blood lost, and the baby's breach position. However, Dr. Albright adds the "C-section" can be performed only if Thelma's vital signs improve. The doctor's mood turned somber as he continues with his diagnosis saying, "If your wife's vital signs don't improve, your son has the best chance. However, with a stronger blood pressure we would have a better chance at saving the both of them." Sensing that Albert is absorbing each word as if though they were scoring punches thrown by a heavy weight boxer, the doctor tries to soften matters by informing Albert that he has approximately one to two hours before a concrete decision will have to be made.

Nonetheless, Albert's face becomes emotionless as he listens to the doctor speak. About this time Albert's state of mind can best be described as that of someone who has awaken from a bad dream just to discover that reality is indeed what he'd hoped was only a dream. Disbelief moves Albert to question, "Doc, you're telling me that if my wife's vital signs don't improve within the next one or two hours I will have to make a decision whether I want my wife or son to live?" Albert snaps, "Is that what you're saying?" He continues, "Well Doc, I can tell you right now it is more important to me that my wife of 19 years be spared opposed to a baby that I could not raise without her anyway."

Dr. Albright pauses for a minute. Then through a soft but composed voice states, "I understand your point of view." He adds, "Mr. Thompson, you still have some time to think this thing through, but in the meantime my staff and I will do the very best we can." The doctor concludes saying, "Mr. Thompson, believe me when I say miracles do happen." After that statement Dr. Albright turns and walks out of the room, down the hall back into the delivery room.

Albert drops his head and walks aimlessly over to a window and begins to stare out through tear-filled eyes, contemplating a decision he hopes he doesn't have to make. However two distractions prevent him from dwelling on any thought for any length of time. One is the sound of the clock on the wall indicating 7:30 p.m., the other is L.T. pulling on his coattail. So Albert does the fatherly thing, and he ignores the clock and gives his attention to his son. L.T. brings his father out of his daze by persisting that he finish the story about the origins of his name(s). Albert sees this as a perfect opportunity to perhaps soothe both of them by shifting their thoughts to an upbeat topic. So with that thought in mind, he decides to share and discuss with L.T. the accomplishments of the men after whom he is named.

Momentarily, without warning a thunder and lightening effect passes throughout Albert's body! He feels an unexplainable calm come over him, a sense of relief he has never felt before! Suddenly a vision flashes before Albert's eyes—the scene of a dove that has an olive twig between its beak flying over an apparent burning bush! Now he is to feel this exhilarating feeling and see this captivating vision once again, but not for years to come. Even though he has been moved by the Holy Spirit and a vision likewise, if Albert knew all of what was to take place it would have moved him to unthinkable joy.

Now this astonishing experience prompts Albert to feel both educational and informative. Therefore he decides to first share and discuss some myths with L.T. that he will certainly encounter solely because L.T. is an African-American. Before informing L.T. of the plights and achievements of each man after whom he was named, a skeptical Albert feels that the following pieces of information and advice are both unfortunate but necessary. Furthermore the importance of each point must be presented and discussed in such a manner it is never forgotten. If introduced properly Albert hoped to answer any questions L.T. might be urged to ask, whereby preparing L.T. for a future that is surely to contain numerous myths. Albert pauses for a moment at which time L.T.'s body language caught his attention. It could be described as hypnotic.

Albert knows that now is the time to begin so he says, "Son what I am about to tell you must never be forgotten. It's wrong to think blacks will always wish the best for you. Just as it is wrong to think that every white person will always wish the worst for you." Albert continues, "Now what I mean is this: each and everyone you meet you must judge that person as one and not think of him or her as a group, whether he is black or white." To ensure he had L.T.'s attention Albert asks, "Do you understand what I mean?" L.T. nods as if to motion go ahead, don't stop! Albert adds, "Now there are some things people say about other races that are not always true, and those untruths are called myths. You see son, a myth is nothing more than a lie, but it's a lie that has been told so often by so many people that folks start to believe those lies. However, you must understand myths cannot physically stop a man from accomplishing anything he sets his mind to." At this point in their conversation Albert turns so that he and L.T. face one another and for a split second stare into one another's eyes.

Albert then speaks in a voice deeper than usual saying, "There are two particular myths that white people often speak of regarding Blacks. One, Blacks can only obtain fame and notoriety through either music, comedy or sports but not through academics and two, Blacks don't dedicate themselves to the point where they're driven to success." Having enlightened L.T. of these myths yet from the tranquil appearance etched upon his little dark brown face, Albert feels that now is the right time to start explaining his sons's name. L.T.'s round eyes are aglow and his ears are tuned in on his father like a trained hawk—at this moment nothing else in the world matters to him. On the contrary for Albert only the years of trials and tribulations he and Thelma have shared matters, but for some unexplainable reason he feels everything is going to be alright. Albert continues, "Now your great-great-grandfather was a slave and he belonged to an owner or in those days they were called masters.

"His name was Master Brown. He owned over 150 slaves and over 200 acres of land. On his land that was in Maryland, Master Brown had many different crops planted. There were over 50 acres of cotton, 25 acres of tobacco, 50 acres of corn and about 25 acres of soybeans. Depending upon what time of the year, the slaves were made to pick whatever crop that was ripe. The slaves were watched by overseers who were white men who assigned the slaves different jobs. Some slaves would have to pick cotton into long bags that were worn on their backs and weighed as much as 100 pounds when completely full. Still, others would have to take those bags over to a wagon and empty them or pile them up. When tobacco and other crops were ready to harvest, it was the same routine. Most of the time the slaves worked from sunup until sundown. During the workday they rarely had a rest break. All the men, women, and children would work these hours regardless of the weather condition."

L.T. asks, "But Daddy didn't the children have to go to school?"

Up until now Albert tried his best to pick his words carefully but can not in this instance, so he answers straightforward saying, "Son back in those days black children didn't attend school and were not allowed to learn nothing but what a white person told them." This information shocks L.T. so much that he lowers his head down to the floor then raises his eyes upward at his father, a look of confusion blankets his face.

Innocently he asks, "But why Daddy?"

Albert, who's searching for ways to show his son how solutions are within the problems, replies, "You see son this is where your great-great-granddaddy was different from most of the other slaves. He always volunteered to be first at doing different jobs. He thought by doing so the overseers and the master would come to know him from the rest of the slaves."

After a brief pause Albert questions, "Do you know something son?"

"What?" shouts L.T.

Albert continues saying, "One day they did notice him."

Again L.T. shouts his approval, "Alright granddaddy!"

Albert continues telling how granddaddy got his wish to be recognized and become a house servant. At the big house granddaddy would assist the maid and do manly chores, then whenever the master and his wife went on trips he would drive the horses and act as their body-guard. Long before granddaddy was chosen to work in the big house he listened closely to how white people talked, read books and especially how they would use numbers. It fascinated granddaddy how the master and overseers came up with the answers that required numbers. There-fore he figured the best way to learn was to watch them whenever they read, or counted, paying close attention to how they shaped their mouth when reading aloud. He started practicing late at night whenever he was alone. Albert adds, "One day he was so intense while practicing rather loud but was so good at reading and counting he got caught."

"Oh-no!" L.T. shouted.

"But it was by the maid who he eventually married," Albert states. L.T. places his right hand over his heart and lets out a big sigh of relief. "Great great-granddaddy was so happy he could read and solve arithmetic problems, he began to sneak books from the Browns' library, where at home he would read them to your great-great-grandmother which she enjoyed so much, that she eventually began reading also.

"Now occasionally granddaddy's speech would slip while in the presence of the master and his wife."

"How?" L.T. asks.

Albert continues, "From time to time granddaddy would speak in a very educated manner—something slaves were not supposed to do. But each time he had done so he'd quickly act as if nothing had happened by saying 'Yes sa, Master Brown,' the way slaves were supposed to talk and the master and his wife would then overlook the incident. After years and years of having taught himself to read, write, and add numbers, granddaddy decided to make a stand for once in his life. Having educated himself but still required to act like what he referred to as less than a man made granddaddy very upset."

Albert adds, "Your great-great-grandfather felt a need like all people that become achievers in life and that need is fueled by sayings like, 'If a man doesn't believe in something strong enough to die for, then he is not fit to live.'"

L.T. went, "Wow!"

Albert adds, "This belief is what led to the incident that caused granddaddy's death. About eight years after my grandfather (Albert's grandpa) was born and his sister was five years old. Granddaddy one day asked his master in front of Papa (Albert's father whom L.T. calls Papa) who was just a little boy at the time, if he could change his family's last name to Thompson. In those days slaves were said to have their masters last name, if they had a name. Master Brown was in shock and asked, 'What did you say boy?' Granddaddy repeated himself!

"Now after the second request old master Brown thought he would get slick. So he walked over and pulled out a piece of paper and a pencil from a desk drawer then told granddaddy, 'Boy, if you can write Thompson on this paper neat and correctly then yes you can change your last name.' So without hesitation grandfather walked over to the desk and took hold of the pencil in his left hand and as pretty as you pleased wrote Herbert

Thompson as clear as day. The master became hysterical. He knew that this meant that granddaddy could read just like he and his wife suspected all along. He immediately ordered the overseers to take great, great-grandfather out and hang him, so about five overseers rushed in and grabbed granddaddy. He didn't try to run or fight but before they took him out of master Brown's sight, great-great-granddaddy asked if he could say one last word, to which the master agreed.

"Standing there in the grasps of those overseers granddaddy looked Master Brown directly into his eyes and said, 'I just want you to know one thing—you did not trick me. I was committed beyond the threat of death to make a name for me and my family.'

"'Are you finished?' asked Master Brown.

"'Yes, I am William,' replied granddaddy. Master Brown looked at him with a puzzled look. He could see that granddaddy no longer feared him but simply looked at him as just another man of equal stature and dignity. Afterwards the overseers took granddaddy out and hung him from the same old oak tree that many other slaves had been hung in the past.

"Later that night while great-great-grandmother was crying, my grandpa told her exactly what had happened earlier. Once he finished all the details great-great grandmother stopped crying, dried her eyes then told grandpa and his sister that from that night on their last name was Thompson." Albert finishes by stating, "And that, my son, is how the family name became Thompson." L.T. begins clapping his hands out of control, then pleads for Albert to tell him why he was named Taliaferro.

Moving along Albert begins again, "Now your middle name came from a famous man named Booker T. Washington. The 'T' stands for Taliaferro. At one point during his life around the time of slavery or better yet after the end of the Civil War, Booker T. began to gain some notoriety as a leader of the Negro race."

That statement prompted L.T. to ask, "Daddy, you mean he was their president?"

To which Albert replies, "Not quite president, but more like their spokesperson. You see when white Americans freed the slaves they didn't have any formal education. This made it hard for slaves to leave the plantation of their former masters, so many of them ended up living and working on the plantations. Now you see Booker T. set out to educate his people so that they could live a better life than what they had before. He wanted to teach them about all the important things in life. Booker T. Washington believed that few things help an individual more than to place responsibility upon him, and to let him know you trust him. Booker T. hoped to provide blacks with the kind of knowledge that would arm them with a certain kind of power. For example anyone who knows the power and importance of political and social contacts means having influence as to what laws are passed."

Albert continues, "For instance, say you're a man and some people want to pass a law that you don't like or think is fair, then with this political influence that Booker T. spoke of someone could prevent that particular law from passing. Booker T. was most famous for the school that he founded."

L.T. shouts, "A school?"

Albert replies, "Yes son, a school. He opened it in July 1881. At that time it had only two buildings but it grew to become a college. Today that college is Tuskegee Institute. The college was for Black children. Booker T. believed that Black kids could learn just as much as whites kids, and by doing so would make them equal in every way. Now at this college, with help from his friends and one man in particular whose name was George Washington Carver, black children were taught everything from reading, writing, arithmetic as well as how to eat and act in public and even how to grow food. Everything needed in order to better their lives was taught in detail at this college."

L.T. then asks, "How long did that take?"

Albert answers, "Son, Booker T. spent the majority of his life in some way or another teaching and speaking in behalf of bettering life for all Americans."

Carefully L.T. asks, "You mean he's dead too?"

"Yes son, I am afraid he is," Albert replied.

Again saddened by the news L.T. lowers his head in sorrow.

With a quick evaluation of the situation Albert manages to perk L.T. up and says, "Now Booker T. had a famous saying of his own that he believed in too- just like great-great-granddaddy."

L.T. eagerly questions, "He did?" then asks, "What was it Daddy?"

Albert answers, "Blacks can be as separate as the fingers yet be as one as the hand."

L.T. shouts "Wow!" and he then begins to work his fingers.

Now totality hypnotized L.T. asks, "What about my first name Luther?"

To which his father replies, "Oh boy now there was a man! Your name Luther comes from a man named Dr. Martin Luther King Jr."

L.T. quickly responds saying, "I know him. We've got a picture of him on our wall in my classroom, he led a lot of people one time."

Albert corrects L.T. saying, "It wasn't just one time— he led people quite often. You see son, Dr. King came onto the scene years after Booker T. and he too was known in his days as a spokesperson for the Black race. As a matter of fact, he would sometimes refer to himself as the drum major for justice."

L.T. quickly jumps on that statement asking, "What's a drum major?"

Albert had anticipated that question and replies, "You see whenever a marching band is playing and marching in a parade, the person out front wearing the tall hat and carrying the long baton is known as the drum major."

This drum major idea sounds neat to L.T. who shows his agreement by saying, "Alright and I'm named after him!" Albert breaks into a little smile and nods his head suggesting yes.

Albert continues, "Now Dr. King's life wasn't easy though—threats were made on him and his family's lives an awful lot of times."

Again L.T.'s little brown face read like a question.

Albert attempting to answer that unspoken question says, "You see son Dr. King's speaking out to whites while leading Blacks in marches and so called rallies did not set too well with many white people in those days. During that time in American history the country was governed by Jim Crow laws."

The name of these laws moves L.T. to repeat, "Jim Crow laws! Daddy, what kind of laws were those?"

Albert answers, "They were supposed to have been separate but equal. Blacks only drink and eat from places that read 'blacks only' while white people did the same. The public facilities for Blacks were always dirty and weren't even half as clean as the ones white people used. And if there was some place where both races were together, for example, the movies or riding on a bus, Blacks would have to stand or sit where ever whites were not."

This noticeable difference in treatment and standards prompts L.T. to ask, "Why Daddy?"

Albert replies, "Now that's the same question Dr. King and other Blacks asked." He adds, "These and other unfair acts were carried out at Blacks' expense all over this country, but one day something happened that sparked a fire deep within a number of black folks. One day on a bus in Alabama a Black woman named Rosa Parks refused to give up her seat to a white man due to the fact she had worked all day long, her feet hurt, and she was tired and refused to be treated unfairly any longer. Regardless the bus driver called the police and they came and arrested her."

L.T. shouts, "Why would they put her in jail for something like that?"

"You see son," Albert continues, "'Jim Crow' meant Blacks were supposed to sit in the back of the bus, and then give up their seat if a white person needed it. That is why today if you see three white people riding in a car, all three of them are sitting in the front seat because they don't like riding in the backseat of a car they call it 'Riding Nigger.'

"Now you see what kind of a job Dr. King was referring to when he called himself the drum major for justice. He spent a big part of his life, even gave his life to the cause of justice for all, but particularly blacks, since they were treated so unfairly. Due to Mrs. Park's, arrest the Blacks in Alabama voted him as their speaker one night at a meeting. Now after they voted him their leader Dr. King told the Black people, 'If I am to be your leader you must follow certain rules.'"

L.T. asks, "What are those rules Daddy?"

Albert replies, "Well son, a few of them were if white people hit or even kicked a Black, they were not to hit or kick back."

This rule made L.T. once again raise his eyes as if in question. Albert continues with another rule, "No matter what white people said to you, as a Black you were not to say it back at them, or repeat any bad action whatsoever." The ideology contained within this statement moves L.T. to raise more than an eyebrow.

Therefore he asks, "Why Daddy?"

Albert explains, "Dr. King believed in nonviolence. He wanted Blacks to win white people's love and compassion, therefore he believed the only way to accomplish this feat was to never fight them physically. Now never fight means to fight with knives, guns and other weapons, but to fight back nonviolently by praying, marching, and discussing the complaints that blacks had with whites. This didn't mean that Dr. King did not go to jail or that he wasn't a victim of numerous injustices. Dr. King never fought back with violence he fought back with books."

L.T. shouts, "Books! You can't fight with books daddy, you read books."

While fighting off the urge to laugh, Albert replies, "Dr. King would read the Bible and books of law. Then he would use what was written in them to fight Jim Crow laws while appealing to whites' conscious. For example, it is written that all men are created equal, but whites weren't treating Blacks equal. The Bible's golden rule reads, 'Do unto others as you would have them do unto you.'

"So you see," Albert continues saying, "These and other phrases would serve as the weapons Dr. King fought whites with instead of violence."

L.T. shouts, "That's neat! Dr. King is known for his famous speeches too!"

Albert exclaims, "Now the march on Washington D.C. and the speech he made was what you meant when you said he led a lot of people one time. In August of 1964, Dr. King led what was called the march on Washington, and on the steps in front of the statue of President Abe Lincoln, he gave his famous 'I Have a Dream' speech. Boy I'll never forget it." Now as Albert speaks he looks up to a corner of that waiting room, as if to say he remembers the time. Albert goes on telling L.T., "Yeah that day Dr. King woke up some folks! In that speech he says, 'I still have a dream. It is deeply rooted in the American dream. I have a dream that one day my four little children will live in a nation where they will not be judged by the color of their skin but by the content of their character.'" Albert pauses for a minute then adds, "Wow!"

Now totally spellbound, L.T. did not know that so much history belonged to blacks, much less was contained within his name. Albert, not knowing of the fire that he has ignited within his son keeps on talking. Having arrived at a point he wants L.T. to understand clearly Albert says, "Son, now Dr.King had a motto that he too believed in strong enough to die for also."

L.T. is like a pit bull waiting for a steak requesting to hear that motto. "What was the motto Daddy, what?" L.T. asks anxiously!

Albert answers, "One day when Dr. King was a little boy about your age he discovered that he wasn't allowed to play with his white friends anymore simply because they were white. Now his mother tried to explain to him in a way that would not hurt his feelings, so she told him these words, 'You are as good as anyone.' Upon hearing these words as a little boy Dr. King lived the rest of his life as good as anyone." Albert then says, "There you have the story, my son, as to why you are named Luther Taliaferro Thompson."

Little does Albert know that the ending of his story was actually the beginning of yet another. And not a moment too soon does Albert finish, when Dr. Albright bursts into the waiting room shouting, "It's a boy and all is well!" As Dr. Albright walks towards Albert, tears fill the wells of his eyes and he shouts, "That's right Mr. Thompson. Congratulations and good luck with your new born son! It was a God sent miracle how quickly your wife's vital signs returned to a safe range. I mean there is no medical explanation for it."

At this time Albert is just all choked up with joy and excitement. He turns to L.T. and asks, "Son what should we name your baby brother?"

L.T., who's now in such a tranquil state of mind, has just one focus and that is to get some books to learn even more black culture and feats of the men he's named after. L.T., so caught up in this hypnotic discovery, speaks out and unintentionally answers Albert's question, by saying, "To books," which Albert hears as Toby.

Albert replies, "Toby, Toby yeah that's a good name son, we'll name him Toby."

2 *FROM THIS MOMENT ON*

It's unfortunate yet true that some blacks become our own worst enemies. However, when one proves himself worthy to lead he's often called Uncle Tom or some other silly description in an attempt to show disrespect for Blacks who achieve something in America. Such is due in part to a form of societal notions.

What are those? That's preconceived positioning that places people in the positions they are supposed to occupy, mostly in regards to race and sex. Highlighting the unexpected is exactly what the Black society should be doing. Telling young black children they can and should achieve much in America in spite of racism and not that they can't achieve anything because of racism.

The truth is young people often grow up to be exactly what they hear early in their lives that they can or will be. That's why it is so important for them to get the right message early. If young black boys are told they can grow up to be doctors and lawyers, half the black folks within earshot would laugh and shout, "Get real." And that is precisely the kind of disbelieving attitude that made it so difficult for some people to accept that a lawyer and doctor were married on the Cosby Show. And it's the same disbelief that stifles initiative among many young black people today.

The people who preach about the reality of racism to young blacks but fail to couple it with a positive message to work hard and achieve despite racism are doing the entire race a disservice. It comes home to roost in the form of a lack of initiative among some poor youths who are without strong parental guidance, i.e., role models.

Our early national heroes were warriors and soldiers, whose acts expressed the pioneer spirit that define the nation. George Washington, Davy Crockett, and Daniel Boone were larger than life figures who captured the public imagination. In modern times, our role models have come to us through various popular forms of news services eager to manufacture and exaggerate. When an electrified press created a single America of instantaneous shared experience through radio and then television, our expectations of our role models changed as well. We now draw them from a larger, more diverse population, celebrating special achievements in sports or business as much as yesterday's heroics in nation building and in war.

While yesterday's role models won freedom for the nation, Dr. King, Booker T. Washington and the likes wrested freedom from the nation for the descendants of the nation's slaves. Therefore in regards to role models no one should underestimate the seriousness or long term effects of the many wounds America has inflicted upon itself since obtaining her independence.

Upon returning home, Albert and L.T. are indirectly greeted by Sara and her so called posse, who are in the living room slouching over the worn furniture. The Thompsons' oldest daughter Sara is 13 years old and wants the world to take notice. She stands approximately 5'6" with almond-shaped light brown eyes and a shapely lanky frame, supported by big feet. Sara wears her medium length black hair pulled back in a ponytail with a covering over the twisted end most of the time, while sporting bangs that are combed up away from her forehead. She prefers to wear her clothes baggy. Sara is not a bad girl, she just hangs around with girls that will smoke and drink anything. Albert believes that if she doesn't change friends, one day her so called posse will have her doing as the pack does. But of course Sara vehemently denies that remark! Sara is strong-willed and Lord knows Thelma preaches to her nonstop as to how a lady carries herself.

It isn't long after Albert and L.T.'s arrival before Albert and Sara get into a disagreement regarding the manner in which she has spent her time at home, while the three of them were at the hospital. In a rather loud and forceful tone, Albert lets Sara know that her simply washing dishes wasn't all that needed to be done, regarding the topic cleaning the entire house. Sara respectfully replies, "Only the dishes and kitchen floor (where Thelma had bled) were the areas that needed cleaning." She added, "After cleaning I went over next door to Mrs. Shirley's and picked up Pamela to look after her until bedtime." Once Sara informs Albert about picking up Pam even though the posse was visiting their argument came to an end. Albert walks over and put his arms around her and apologizes for jumping the gun. She accepts then tells him it was just stress. Sara then suggests that maybe he should take a warm shower and get in bed for the night, which is just what Albert proceeds to do.

Meanwhile L.T. who is still on fire from his father's in depth storytelling goes directly over to the family's magazine rack, where he finds the *Ebony* with Dr. King's picture on the cover. L.T. picks it up and gazes in awe. He then takes the magazine into his and Jason's room where he lays across his bed and slowly turns through the various pages looking for Dr. King's picture on each. Suddenly there appears a long article about Dr. King which L.T. attempts to read as best he can. However, the more L.T. reads the sharper each imaginary picture appears within the window of his mind. L.T.'s mind being that of an eight-year-old, he begins to flick back and forth as most kids his age will do while reading. In this case his mind goes through imaginary stages ranging from the wild (he is one of Dr. King's children) to the not so wild (he might one day accomplish something in his life that would place him in the same class as Dr.King).

L.T. is his parents third child or, as his mother refers to him, her middle baby, a title that is true more now than before his brother's birth. L.T. now has a brother and sister older than he and a sister and brother younger than him also. Now L.T. is the one child that his parents seem to forget, not actually forget, but he's the one they have to speak to the least. He never has to be reminded of his one household chore to empty the trash nor do L.T.'s parents give a second thought about him doing his homework nightly. Needless to say, his report card and overall mannerisms would make any parent proud.

However, living in the ghetto does require a stern disposition not to be persuaded by the usual everyday activities. (Gangs, dope taking and dealings, prostitution, etc....) Needless to say ghetto kids usually face peer pressure so often until a realistic amount can't even be imagined. L.T. is no exception to this frightening dilemma. On the other hand, L.T. is different in that routine events within his neighborhood have not yet tainted him. L.T. is different in that sports is not his planned avenue of escape from poverty and obscurity. Instead his hopes lie squarely on educational channels. L.T. is so shy he doesn't even try to dance, he prefers listening to reggae instead of rap music, and he chooses conventional haircuts over the modern styles worn by today's youths. The majority of the time L.T. thinks and acts much older than his actual age. Now it is not known for sure why sports don't interest L.T. because Albert has introduced him and his older brother Jason to the three major sports numerous times, but in L.T.'s case it has been to no avail.

On the other hand anyone who wishes to examine the essence of school or is willing to discuss any process for learning is what it takes in order to start L.T. talking. At this stage in his young life nothing brings L.T. more happiness than knowing he has not one but three unforgettable role models that no one can ever take from him. Better than that, two of them he can read about anytime he wants, by simply visiting the nearest library. From this moment on L.T. will attempt to become a trailblazer in pursuit of more knowledge. At about 1:00 a.m. L.T. is interrupted from his dreams by a knock on the front door. It's Jason his big brother. Jason hopes that since the light is on in his and L.T.'s room that L.T. will answer the door. Instead it is Dad.

Albert doesn't disappoint Jason. He confronts him with the usual conversation. "Son do you know what time it is?" Albert asks. Before Jason can respond Albert inquires, "Haven't I told you before that just because you're a senior in high school doesn't make you a grown man? For as long as you live in this house you'll be in before midnight even if it is a Friday or Saturday night!" he exclaims.

Jason, sensing that this is one of those times when he must choose his words carefully replies, "Dad I wasn't no place where I could get into any trouble."

Albert vehemently states," But you wasn't home neither!"

Again with much caution Jason says, "Dad you know me and the African Brothers meet on the third Thursday of the month."

Albert's response again echoes his ill feelings regarding Jason's club agenda by saying, "You put more time into that club and meetings than you do into looking for a real job."

It should be noted that Jason believes that if minorities are to under go the much-needed transformation regarding their status as disenfranchised citizens, then they must unite in order to capitalize on opportunities once available. However, the manner as to how such ideology is to be practiced is what he and Pops disagree on. During the course of their conversation, Jason has been edging towards the kitchen with Albert trailing. By this time they have made their way into the kitchen where Jason opens the refrigerator door to discover his plate has not been prepared like Thelma usually does. It's absence prompts Jason to inquire, "What did mama cook for dinner?"

Albert who has taken a seat at the kitchen table, gives him a cold stare. "She didn't cook because she's in the hospital," Albert informs him.

Jason immediately slams the refrigerator door and shouts, "Hospital!"

Albert begins to tell him about the events of the evening. He makes it a point to speak of L.T.'s heroic deeds. Jason pretends not to have heard a single word and anxiously asks, "How is Mama? Is she alright?"

Albert answers, "She had a rough go of it there for awhile but she's fine now."

"What about the baby?" Jason asks.

Albert gets up from the table says, "Oh yeah you have a baby brother and his name is Toby."

Learning of this news Jason shouts, "Alright Dad!" Holding his right hand up in the hi-five position says, "Lay it on me!"

Albert breaks into a smirk and slaps five on Jason. Then while turning for his return trip to bed, Albert says over his left shoulder, "Now your sister has cleaned-up this kitchen, make sure it's clean before you go to bed."

Now alone with his thoughts, Jason can't help but think just for a minute what his family's atmosphere would have become if his mother had died, due to that ambulance not coming. But he refuses to dwell on such a thought, choosing instead to prepare himself a sub sandwich.

Meanwhile, Albert lays in bed. He's now wide awake after his conversation with Jason. He too can't help but reflect back on today's events. While laying flat on his back looking at the bedroom ceiling Albert begins giving thanks to God. He begins saying, "I want to thank you Lord for so many blessings, you've blessed my family and in such a way that it will take a lifetime for me to even attempt to repay you." Albert continues adding, "So at this time in my life I promise that it is a lifetime of service you'll get." Albert is a big dark-skinned man who's distinguishing facial features are accented by his salt and pepper colored hair, while his muscle-toned build warrants respect rather he chooses to unleash a word or not from his booming voice. There is no mistaking the fact that his features resemble those of the Mandingo slaves—a fact he's very proud of indeed.

On the other hand Albert, like his parents before him, preaches to his children about the importance of an education, in particularly a college education. It hurts him deeply that a freak knee injury was the major blow that derailed his efforts and cost him an opportunity for a college degree. Unfortunately he and Thelma, like their parents before them, are financially unable to assist their children in achieving this noteworthy accomplishment. Nonetheless any spare time he gets between his two jobs, Albert will continue preaching to his kids about the importance of proper self-development. He knows that hard work is a requirement for success in life, and there is no substitute. He someday hopes to get this critical point across to his offspring, because in doing so he knows he will have armed them with an awesome tool needed in order to become contributors to society, whereby in their own rights they will be able to shatter myths. Tonight Albert's mind is in search of special insight, roving between giving thanks and praise to God for daily blessings, to reconstruction of his wife and newborn son's miracle event. Equally important is the unthinkable thought of raising his children without Thelma in this house. It should be noted that he and Thelma were married at age 19. Well, Albert was 19 years old. Thelma was only 17 and they've never given any thought to being separated, no matter how hard times have been. At some point during his passionate attempt to both give thanks and unite with God, Albert manages to fall off to sleep.

As the new day dawns, the fresh morning dew covers the ground. Meanwhile on the 7th floor of the hospital Thelma awakens. Naturally she's tired and very sore. It's about 7:20 a.m. She is coherent to her surroundings however, many of yesterday's events are vague. Needless to say, Thelma wants to know the status of her baby. All of the required monitors and equipment indicate that all is stable with her vital signs. The night shift nursing staff is thrilled that she has passed what is considered a crucial time period in such good shape. At this time Thelma presses the call button. Upon the nurse's arrival into the room Thelma requests to see her baby. With understanding, the nurse informs her that it is still too early however, assures Thelma that he is okay and she will see him once she finishes breakfast and the morning routine. Upon hearing these requirements Thelma informs the nurse, "I don't want no breakfast, I just want to see and hold my baby." Again the nurse repeats the hospital rules. Sensing that she is not getting anywhere Thelma changes her stance and begins to insist that she start now washing up and whatever else required to see her baby.

The nurse assists her out of bed and into the bathroom where they begin taking care of Thelma's morning hygiene. Thelma asks, "Does my son have all of his fingers and toes?"

The nurse answers lazily, "Yes he has all of his fingers and toes."

Throughout the procedure Thelma questions the nurse, who in return answers her accordingly. As the two of them emerge from the bathroom to discover Thelma's breakfast at her bedside, she again questions, "Will I get to see my boy when I finish eating?" to which the nurse replies with a definite yes. Thelma eats as quickly as she possibly can, afterwards almost as if it were pre-planned, Albert and Sara enter the room pushing Toby's incubator.

Thelma's eyes light up like lanterns would light up the midnight darkness as she raises up from the bed to see her baby. She gazes at Toby's tiny brown body carefully examining him from head to toe. She wastes little time in reaching into the holes of the incubator to gently stroke Toby's delicate tissue like skin. As she takes in his features, Albert tells her of the proposed name of Toby. Upon hearing it she pauses for a moment then says, "He looks like a Toby." Hospital policy states premature babies can't be out of the nursery longer than thirty continuous minutes at one time. So Thelma says bye-bye to Toby and Sara returns him to the nursery. Albert locates a long tan chair near the window where he sits, the chair is in clear view of his wife who is lying on the bed. When Sara returns she scoots onto the bed next to Thelma.

There they begin discussing in detail yesterday's events. Shortly after the discussion begins, Dr. Albright enters and discovers, to his delight, that all is well. However, he informs them that the next forty-eight hours should greatly clear up both Thelma and Toby's status. The doctor adds that he can possibly send Thelma home in five days. After this statement Sara begins clapping her hands in approval. Dr. Albright wishes everyone a good day and departs. Shortly after the doctor's departure the head nurse comes in and informs Albert and Sara that visiting hours are over, but will start again at 6: 00 p.m. Having to obey the rules Albert and Sara kiss

Thelma. Before they depart, they inform her that Jason will return later with Albert.

Meanwhile today at school L.T. is a symbol of sheer happiness. At every opportunity he shares with his classmates the wealth of information contained within his name. On this particular Friday, L.T. looks at Dr. King's picture on the classroom wall with a new sense of pride and a feeling of personal identity. Throughout the day Mrs. Parker his third grade teacher observes L.T.'s new enthusiastic display of pride and she too hears the accomplishments of his heroic namesakes. These fascinating details move Mrs. Parker to invite L.T. to visit with her during recess so that she may assist him as best she knows how. In her efforts, Mrs. Parker stops by the library prior to recess and checked out a book about famous black leaders. At the beginning of the recess hour, she and L.T. manage to get a seat on one of the benches in view of the class on the playground. At which time Mrs. Parker and L.T. began to discuss and read about the unique fashion in which his name came about. Mrs. Parker informs L.T. that his parents or whomever it was that named him are very clever. L.T. snaps, "It was my daddy!"

Mrs. Parker smiles in agreement, "Then show him the book," and gives him the book she checked out. Of course L.T. wants to know if Booker T. Washington and Dr. King are mentioned.

Naturally she replies, "I checked it out for that reason, so that I could read and discuss these men with you." She then turns to and reads about Booker T. Afterwards Mrs. Parker sees the gleam of pride in L.T.'s eyes, she manages to hold back her tears, even though her eyes were full of water. Mrs. Parker then turns to the pages on Dr. M. L. King, Jr. and reads them aloud as L.T. listens proudly. Upon completion she is moved again but manages not to cry. Mrs. Parker and L.T. then begin a brief discussion during which time L.T. informs her that after school he will go to the library and check out more books about Dr. King and Booker

T. also. Mrs. Parker agrees that he should do just that, then she makes him promise that he will. L.T. immediately promises to do so. She feels certain that the fire of desire burns within L.T. and hopes that it will burn forever. On the other hand Mrs. Parker knows that ghettos are actually combat zones and for L.T. or any child to survive and become a productive adult could be defined as a miracle. Suddenly the bell rings and everyone moves back inside to be released for the day. During his usual walk home L.T. is unmoved by the sights and sounds that surround him. He can't wait to get home and knock out his homework so that he can get to the library and read more about slavery. His arrival home jars his memory of Thelma still in the hospital. He looks into his parents bedroom anyway and of course she isn't there. Without hesitation L.T. begins and finishes his homework and afterwards he grabs a bite to eat. Then he leaves a note on the refrigerator for his dad saying that he's at the library.

Once inside the library L.T. wanders around trying to find books about slavery. When finally he does, he quickly pulls a book from the shelf and buries his head into it. While reading he is shuffling through the library into the seating area where he slides into a chair without even raising his head. There he begins to read as best he can, and for the most part he knows how to pronounce the majority of the words. Even though there are some he can't read, he pronounces them as best he can and continues. The more L.T. reads and learns of both slavery and the history of civil rights, the more meaningful the achievements of men like those he is named after becomes. On and on he reads, sinking deeper and deeper into an irreversible tranquil state of mind that is to fuel his inward personal fire for life. Much to his surprise, the librarian blinks on and off the lights which indicate that the library will be closing in 15 minutes and now is the visitors' last chance to check out books. So L.T. rushes up to the desk and checks out the book he is reading, and then starts for home.

Across town on the seventh floor of the hospital, Albert and Jason are saying good night to Thelma and Toby. Thelma is doing much better. As for Toby the circumcision wasn't any fun, but otherwise he too is doing fine. Shortly after her family leaves her alone with her thoughts, Thelma starts to think. Throughout her life Thelma has been strong and hardly ever sick, and child bearing hasn't been a major problem except of course this time with Toby.

She is a brown-skinned woman with a small head, nose, and ears. However she has large almond-shaped hypnotic brown eyes and full lips. Thelma stands approximately 5'4" feet tall and 140 pounds with a big bust, and long dark brown wavy hair. Her detailed beauty and shapely figure are so embedded that even the birthing of five children hasn't made her lose much of her God-blessed beauty. Thelma, like both her parents, is a deeply religious person. Albert attends church also, but nothing like his wife. At the age of 25, she returned to school and obtained her GED—Thelma felt that she owed it to herself to complete high school, by whatever means necessary. Such display is small evidence of her determination. Once Thelma sets her mind to accomplishing a task, anyone can bet their life on her accomplishing it.

On this particular night after having listened to Albert and the staff talk about just how close she came to losing this battle with life, Thelma wants to thank the Almighty for bringing her and her baby through. Alone in her room, lying in bed with both her eyes and mind traveling at warp speed, she takes time out to pray. Thelma's prayers are so intense that by the time she is done she has broken out into a cold sweat. Afterwards she feels a burning desire to go home. Unfortunately it's about 10:30 p.m. and therefore any chance of her getting discharged is unrealistic. Therefore she begins to reflect back to the days when she and Albert were courting. She can remember it as if it were yesterday how Albert would come over to her parents house and try to bribe her mother and then he'd offer to help her father anyway possible so that he might get to see and talk with her. The few times that his little plan worked nothing happened other than them sharing a few laughs.

Having completed her trip down memory lane, Thelma laughs to herself. She then gets up out of bed per doctor's orders (for assistance with the healing process) and gently walks around the room for a minute or two. Now staring out of the big window, Thelma looks out and upward at the ebony star-filled sky; the pleasant sight brings a smile to her face. Thelma then begins to think in a motherly manner about each of her children. Talking aloud she begins saying, "Lord, my oldest son Jason isn't a bad boy, he is just searching to find himself. You know how kids get at that certain age when they began to smell themselves." Thelma continues saying, "From this moment on I pray that you walk with him, and go before him to make the crooked places straight and make the rough places smooth."

Moving along she states, "My oldest daughter Sara is a sweet girl, and she is good about accomplishing womanly things around the house. But Lord, due to our neighborhood she is forced to be exposed to a lot of wicked things going on, whereby she must find friends from among troubled young ladies. I understand that in the midst of such victimizing circumstances it is easy to be led astray, however with your presence and blessings, Lord I know she'll turn out alright." Thelma continues adding, "Lord as for my middle baby L.T., I lift him up to you in an attempt that you might see the ocean of potential in him. I pray that his many gifts are tapped and used according to your will, and that his heart's desire will always be thou will."

She concludes saying, "Now as for my two little ones Pamela and Toby, I beg that you bless Albert and me to provide for them whatever they need, not necessarily what they want, but all of their needs. For these blessings I pray, Amen." Upon completion of this particular statement Thelma feels an urge to get a good night's sleep. Slowly she lowers her head and eyes from the star-filled sky, turns and shuffles back over to the bed, pausing long enough to say her nightly prayer. Then she gently slides onto the bed where she seems to fall asleep before her head hits the pillow.

3 *PATENTED QUEST*

Everyone knows that we all need a sense of belonging, a sense of welcome, a sense of importance and vitality. Furthermore we all want and need pats on the back, thumbs up every now and then, simple pleasantries, occasional presumed innocence and second chances. Such benefits are appreciated by every kind of human being you can imagine, regardless of color, religion, nationality, age, profession and personality. To be the recipient of praise is as much an energizer to one's self-esteem as the leaf-bearing dove was to Noah.

By and by, four years have passed since the ordeal regarding Toby's birth. Today both he and Thelma have long since put it behind them. It is with unquenchable optimism that L.T. is beginning a fresh start in his young life. Over the years he has been like a man possessed, visiting the Schomberg library after school, while on weekends, visiting from opening until closing. During such time L.T. reads every newspaper and magazine article he possibly can that pertains to the trails of any black pioneer. Recollection of the myths Albert spoke about is the driving force behind all L.T.'s actions. The motivation has been so overpowering until it appears as if L.T. is wearing horse blinders and has plugged his ears with earplugs in an attempt to wipe out any distractions. Furthermore L.T.'s transformation has made him an even better student than before his enlightening encounter. That memorable educational awakening has played a major part in his change in attitude, study habits, and the increase in L.T.'s reading comprehension and speed. Even his math skills are sharper.

Now 12 years of age L.T.'s mental sky is one that is vividly colored but happens to be constantly engaged in an unseen tug-of-war, due to his observation of a reality that has only one suitable color—black. This tug-of-war is triggered in part by what his mind advises him to do whenever he's confronted with real life problems that challenge his desire to stand steadfast in his psychological belief. Such belief echoes this phrase, "Concrete gains can only be achieved through commitment and dedication."

However, before life's investments can be made, certain factors must be weighed. It must be thoroughly understood everything worthwhile has it's price. Along the same line, should calculated planning take place from the onset of all critical investments, most likely the dividends will reap windfall profits. In L.T.'s case such strategy could serve as an ideal plan for reference as he continues to experience changes in life that threaten his enthusiasm. Throughout life the winds of change may buffet a soul. At some points, change is certain even if it is not clear what direction the change will take. In spite of the inevitable, people have to start with the basic in order to move on to more complex things. Practicing such ideology combined with shrewd behavior has kept L.T. free from the unscrupulous Lazerbeam, the territorial drug dealer. Lazerbeam has been trying to recruit L.T. but to no avail. However, another worthless menace to society takes shape in the form of Anthony Bates, a gang leader who has also been pressuring L.T. to join his gang. But again L.T. has not succumbed to the tactics.

A relentless desire to shatter as many myths as possible provides L.T. with the only means of ammunition whenever he is confronted by either of his adversaries. Even though he does not have any physical weapons with which to fight, L.T. more than makes up for any shortcomings through divine guidance, whereby it results in maximum use of his mental strength. L.T. knows full well that it's almost impossible to escape his adversaries twenty-four hours a day, seven days a week, so occasionally he doesn't even try. Besides he need not give ideas for eluding them any special attention nor must he change his habits in order to do so because once L.T. arrives at his destination which is usually home, the library, or school, they aren't interested in entering anyway.

However today L.T. is bubbling over with anticipation because tonight at 7:00 p.m. he hopes to view Dr.King's famous "I Have A Dream" speech that is to be shown at the library. But first he must deal with a pressing issue—that is to get away from Lazerbeam who is leaning against the fence on the corner which L.T. is approaching. Lazerbeam looks as if though L.T. is the one person he's waiting for. Upon L.T.'s arrival at the corner, Lazerbeam reaches out and catches hold of his left arm just enough to stop him. Lazerbeam immediately begins to try and entice L.T. First he reaches into his left front pocket and pulls out a knot that consists of 50 and 100 dollar bills which he shows to L.T. Lazerbeam then refers to L.T. by the personal nickname he calls him. "Say Little Einstein, you think you can count this much money?" Lazerbeam asks.

"Yes and you could too if you studied math sometimes," L.T. replies.

"Oh you're a real bookworm, huh?" Lazerbeam inquires.

L.T. replies, "Every minute of each day I can study, I do."

Pretending not to have heard L.T.'s last remark, Lazerbeam reaches into his left coat pocket and pulls out a matchbox filled with drugs (crack). Then while pushing the matchbox towards L.T., Lazerbeam says, "Hey Little Einstein, if you really want to upgrade your math skills, and perhaps even buy yourself some adequate study material, I can help you. Just deliver this package to the third floor of that complex." He points to a run-down building about one block away, "To a brother named Big Al." Lazerbeam then waves the knot in L.T.'s face and he adds, "I'll give you two of these 50's (dollar bills) for your Einstein time."

Now L.T. studies the money. "100 dollars," he says under his breath. Momentarily he envisions owning a reference book like those he's fascinated by in the library's reference section.

Almost as if he reads L.T.'s mind Lazerbeam says, "These crispy 50's could buy some mighty fine reference books for research projects."

For some unexplainable reason this comment has a melodious sound as it enters L.T.'s ears. Persuasion is about to get the best of him, when suddenly the jarring sound of a siren kickstarts L.T's common sense whereby the myths his father spoke of bolt to the forefront of his mind. Having regained his composure, L.T. looks Lazerbeam straight into his eyes and says, "If you really knew the true value of both time and money, you wouldn't spend yours in the manner that you do." Upon completion

L.T. breaks and runs across the street! He nearly gets hit by a speeding car!

Once he gets home it's business as usual. He speaks to his mother then completes his homework assignments in that order. Afterwards he spends a few minutes of playtime with Pamela and Toby until dinnertime. Now that dinner is over, it's off to the library. Oh boy! L.T. is really excited because he has heard a lot about Dr.King's famous speech and he has even read it numerous times. But unfortunately due to a number of circumstances within his life that for all practical purposes has robbed L.T. of an opportunity to feel the heat via television, this is his first chance to witness the historical events of that memorable day.

Now as L.T. approaches the library, he's surprised that there isn't a line. All day he thought there would be such a long line. Then suddenly he thinks to himself that maybe he is late! They started showing the movie earlier, so his heart starts to pound fast. As he runs it pounds even faster until he gets inside and discovers that the library looks the same. Matter of fact he soon learns that nobody's even in the movie room yet—the showing is supposed to start in about twenty minutes. The television and VCR are set up to show the speech but L.T. seems to be the only person interested in the showing. So he thinks to himself that maybe when the showing starts more people will show up. With a little time to spare, he browses through the library's reference section. Needless to say this is his favorite section even though he knows that these books can't be checked out.

It's now time for the showing so L.T. moves on into the viewing room where he discovers that he and perhaps forty others are interested enough to come together and amplify this historical event. The librarian enters the room. She doesn't even give the number in attendance a second look as she turns on the TV set then starts the VCR and takes a seat in the back. L.T. of course is seated in the front row. As the tape plays L.T.'s little heart flutters with pride as he witnesses the agenda of that memorable day in Washington DC. His eyes simultaneously examine the other patrons while absorbing the images and sounds that are being projected from the TV screen. After a short time L.T. begins to watch so intensely that he, like many in attendance at the rally, begins to sweat. He fans himself as often as anyone of the approximately 250 thousand folks in attendance at the monument. Once Dr. King begins to speak the best description of the impact of his words upon L.T.'s body is to say, each word had an etching effect.

After the movie ends a perplexed L.T. exits the library and begins to walk home. But now confused, he wonders aloud to himself, "How in the world could it be, that all of the history derived from that rally's events, has not moved the entire black population in such a manner that they would never forget?" As for himself, just hearing Dr. King's speech alone served as an injection of unflappable identity which on this night (in L.T.'s mind) develops between him and Dr. King. Continuing to evaluate the rally's agenda prompts more questions from within L.T. which he examines while in a discussion with himself. L.T. inquires, "Why didn't the black parents of those days make it a point to educate their children of the possible benefits that type of gathering could produce?" He then reasons aloud, "That's why daddy schooled me about my historical namesakes." With admiration L.T. adds, "Now that I know of their treasured achievements, my daddy knows that I'm going to take pride in guarding the jewels found within my treasurable name."

Needless to say, L.T. speaks only for himself about the way in which the various reasons behind the march on Washington D.C. affect him. Still quite young, he is unaware of the many hurdles and resistances blacks have had to overcome since that time frame of American history. Nevertheless this experience has served as wood to the fire that presently burns within him. On the contrary, time and circumstances have produced many more Anthony Bates and gang members, than would-be Dr.King's—a fact L.T. is certain to discover once he turns this next corner.

"Boom" a right, "Blam" a left, then suddenly about 12 more rights, and left combinations land in numerous locations upon L.T.'s skinny body until he can't stand up any longer. Shortly after he falls, Anthony the bully stands over L.T. who's curled up into a fetal position for the best possible protection. During this time the bully speaks to L.T. saying, "I see your self-found righteousness can't save you from reality!" He continues by asking L.T., "What do you have to say for yourself now?"

Through a series of moans and groans L.T. replies, "I am still going to include you in both my prayers and quest for a unified black society, brother."

Due to this expected yet not understood statement by L.T., the bully begins laughing and steps clear of him. He then orders his gang to, "Let's go and leave the professor to read up on how to give himself first-aid." They all are laughing as they leave a stunned L.T. groaning in pain. He manages to get on his feet and regain his composure and continues on toward's home. Suddenly L.T. recalls with excitement Dr. King's philosophy referring to fighting his enemies with books and nonviolence. A burst of excitement is brought about in part when L.T. suddenly realizes that through books and nonviolence was how he too fought his enemies tonight.

Now it's one week later and on this particular Friday morning, L.T. gets up earlier than usual for school. Since this school year is about to end he has decided to try and get a summer job. Due to the fact that he is only twelve years old, L.T. knows he'll have to come up with a clever idea if someone is to even notice or, better yet, hire him. "Wow!" Like a quick kick to the seat of his pants he's got it. L.T. has decided that he'll make himself an "A" shape sign just like those used in Dr. King's day, and it'll read "Every good man deserves a job." He has also decided that he is going to march up and down the streets of Manhattan while wearing his sign until he gets hired. But for now he's got to get to school. Ms. Johnson doesn't play being late to class. Throughout this day L.T.'s mind runs one hundred miles a minute until around 2 p.m. when L.T. asks his teacher for permission to go to the bookstore. With her permission he sprints down to the bookstore and buys two white poster boards and a blue marker, needed supplies.

Upon returning from the bookstore and back in his seat, L.T. starts his usual routine of staring out of the window in the direction of Edison, the predominately white middle school. It's not that L.T. stares out the window instead of doing his schoolwork. He only stares out the window when he has finished his assignments or at times when his mind is over flowing with ideas, like now. There's only two weeks of school remaining in this year and since L.T. has been on the honor roll the entire year, there is no doubt he'll be promoted. Slowly he pulls back on his daydreaming of the future to the present. Shortly after having done so, the bell rings signaling the end of both today's classes and the week. Quickly L.T. gathers up his belongings and scats out of the classroom even before Ms. Johnson can get a word to him. He's not in the mood today to deal with Lazerbeam or Anthony and his gang so L.T. takes the long but safest route in an attempt to avoid them, which he does.

Once home L.T. loudly announces his presence shouting, "Mama I'm home." But today Thelma signals for him to be quiet because his younger sister and brother are asleep. L.T. catches the signal and begins to tiptoe as quietly as possible into his and Jason's bedroom, where he immediately starts on his employment sign. First he gathers up the needed materials; a pair of scissors, two poster boards, blue marker, a clothes hanger and some kite string. L.T. then goes over and clears off the top of the dresser drawer to create a central work place. Then he writes his slogan "Every Good Man Deserves A Job" on both posters. Now he takes the kite string, measures and cuts it into two even pieces so that once they are tied between the posters his signs will hang even both in front and in back. L.T. continues by using the clothes hanger; he punches holes near the top edges of the boards, then runs the string through them and ties a knot into each side. Thereby when worn the sign can be read from both the front and back views. L.T. then picks up and pulls the front poster over his head as the back one falls against his back. He looks into the mirror and likes what he sees. Then while pumping his fist, he lets out a moderately loud "alright." He then removes the sign, lays it onto a chair and cleans up after himself.

After dinner it's back to the Schomburg Center—its got the best of everything; books, study tables, computers, and the head librarian Mrs. Hepburn is always willing to help anyone. This evening upon his arrival L.T. is greeted by Mrs. Hepburn and the special nickname which she refers to him, "Mr. Owl." L.T. blushes and returns her greeting. He usually goes directly to the reference section then chooses the book he has been reading if he hasn't finished.

Now L.T. doesn't know that Mrs. Hepburn has noticed some of the many unique qualities he possesses. Mrs. Hepburn is approximately 43 years old and she has those librarian features. She stands about 5'1" has a medium build, oversized bust, and graying black hair. She wears her eye glasses on a chain around her neck. They are the kind that most people who wear them, seem to look out over the top rather than through. Nevertheless she can't help but admire L.T. and his determination. She knows of the neighborhood in which he lives and that it doesn't stop him from visiting in any type of weather. Even though a large number of people visit this library, L.T.'s presence stands out to her and once he arrives his little mind is like a sponge trying to absorb everything within his grasp whether he comes into direct contact with the various material or merely hears of it in passing.

Mrs. Hepburn can clearly see that this kid is driven, by what or whom she isn't sure. Nonetheless one thing is certain—she's going to assist him in anyway possible with hopes that he achieves his goals regardless of what they are. During this visit after having been in the library for about an hour, L.T. decides to chat with the librarian. As he approaches she is working on the monthly report at the front desk. After some small talk and a slight indication of attention, L.T. starts in about his rich heritage. Mrs. Hepburn who was half-listening at the start of this little get-acquainted session, has now given L.T. her full attention. At a point that seems appropriate she asks, "Knowing all of this information, is that the one thing that moves you to visit this library like you do?"

L.T. replies, "Yes ma'am no doubt about it!"

Due to this answer Mrs. Hepburn can't help but feel a sigh of relief in knowing that L.T.'s quest for knowledge is genuine and pure. They talk about so many things before either of them knows it, one of the assistant librarians is making the closing announcements. Afterwards Mrs. Hepburn turns to L.T. and says, "Well Mr. Owl, you've managed to do it again; that is, stay until closing."

He states, "Well at least now you know why I stay."

She smiles down at him then says, "Yes I do, and good luck on your job hunt tomorrow."

L.T. replies, "Thank you." He then quickly gathers up his belongings and exits for home.

To L.T. the ringing sound of his alarm clock seems as if it will never happen. Today his quest for a job can be summed up best by this often quoted phrase, "Today is the first day of the rest of your life." Once he has gotten dressed and eaten breakfast, he gets his lunch from the refrigerator, then places a note on its door reminding Thelma of his whereabouts. With his sign under one arm and his lunch in the opposite hand L.T. walks smartly down to the subway station. Having caught the train numerous times before, he goes through the routine of purchasing the token, going through the turnstile and getting on the train in no time.

Once off the train L.T. quickly pulls the top flap of his sign over his head and starts walking. He is heading to Wall Street because he's heard a lot of stories about how millionaires are made everyday on Wall Street. Now on Times Square L.T. begins walking from West 44th street to West 46th, back and forth. As various people pass him some are laughing and others are caught up in their own affairs and don't even notice him at all. Then there are some who give him the thumbs-up sign. L.T. takes them all in stride. After having walked all morning from 9:30 until 12: 00 noon without getting any serious offers, he decides to break thirty minutes for lunch. During his break L.T. brainstorms about that one possibility he knows is out there somewhere. In between daydreaming he finishes off the two peanut butter and jelly sandwiches and the apple his mother packed into his lunch. Afterwards the urge to use the restroom prompts L.T. to go in search of one.

The parking garage directly across the street adjacent to the tinted glass skyscraper building is a good place to start. Therefore, L.T. gathers up his sign and walks down to the crosswalk. Once across the street and into the garage, L.T. cautiously strolls through the maze of cars in search of a men's room. Nearly ten minutes into his search, L.T. notices two boys about his age stealing tires off of a navy blue limousine. They have already removed one of the front tires and are presently working on the other. At first glance L.T. attempts to do as most New Yorkers, to ignore the crime in progress. But for some unexplainable reason he could not allow two boys his age to take a chance on going to jail or worse getting shot by the owner. So he thinks to himself for a moment, then just as two men exit the elevator L.T. begins yelling in the direction of the thieves, "Get the hell away from my uncle's ride you little punks! I'm going to kill both of you!" L.T.'s little prank scares the would-be thieves and they take off running. The two men who exited the elevator are Judge Cromwell and his chauffeur, Charles. The limo happens to belong to the Judge. Once Judge Cromwell and Charles get close enough to talk with L.T., the Judge identifies himself and Charles and thanks L.T. for the heroic act. A shy L.T. states, "It was nothing, I just didn't want to see two more black males get shot or wind up in jail." Meanwhile Charles puts the tires back onto the car.

Judge Cromwell replies, "That's an intelligent way of looking at the situation, and again I want to thank you." He then asks, "What is your name?"

L.T. replies, "Luther Thompson, but everybody calls me L.T. sir."

As L.T. speaks an observant Judge Cromwell notices L.T.'s sign and asks, "Just what type of a job are you looking for L.T.?"

In as a deep a voice as he's able L.T. says, "An honest job with honest pay sir."

The Judge can't help but chuckle but manages to cut it short and says," I like that, I like an honest man." Afterwards he takes out a note pad and pen from inside his right coat pocket and writes his name and address including a date and time on it, tears it off, and gives the note to L.T.

"Judge Cromwell is my name," he adds, "In order for you to get to my home, you must catch the blue line subway. Here is five dollars," he hands L.T. the money. Judge Cromwell adds, "If you want that job, then be at my home on that date and we'll discuss it okay?"

By now L.T.'s gut feelings are telling him this man's alright. L.T. unintentionally shouts back, "Yes sir!" Then adds, "I sure will, you can bet on it." The Judge then says, "Let's shake on it."

L.T. grabs and shakes the Judge's hand almost nonstop but does manage to turn it loose. Afterwards Judge Cromwell turns and get into the limo and Charles drives off.

L.T. can't believe what has just happened! He looks astonishingly at the note and five dollar bill and yells, "Yes, yes sir, millionaires are born on Wall Street everyday." He quickly pulls himself together because by this time it seems to him that people are watching. L.T. starts walking to the subway station. He can use the rest room there so he tucks his sign under his right arm as he picks up his pace. At the substation, L.T. runs quickly into the men's room then buys his token and boards the train. During the trip home he's hardly able to maintain his composure. Once the train stop at his destination, L.T. leaps from the train in a hurry to get home. From the moment L.T. enters the door he informs any one of his family members who'll listen of his adventurous and successful job hunt. Naturally everyone is proud of him and excited as well.

The past week has been one big roller coaster ride and on this Thursday, one day before the end of school, L.T. sits among his sixth grade classmates as their teacher talks to the class. Ms. Johnson is reflecting over the kind of year it has been while informing the class of some things to look forward to in the future. From experience Ms. Johnson knows that most of these children aren't likely to graduate from high school, much less college. You see, Ms. Johnson grew up in Brooklyn over 18 years ago herself and she's well aware of the peer pressure today's youth place upon one another. She has taught in this school district for almost 13 years and most of the time her predictions come true.

Ms. Johnson is 38 years old she stands approximately 5'4" tall, weighs around 135 pounds with a small build. Her features are those of a woman who's natural beauty is so defined that she doesn't even need to wear any make-up to please the eye. She has smooth brown skin with shoulder length auburn colored wavy hair. Her hazel colored eyes are oval shaped, they compliment her shapely figure in the same manner that Isotoner gloves fit a lady's hands. Needless to say Ms. Johnson can easily pass for years younger than her actual age. Unfortunately she is widowed because three years ago her husband was killed in an automobile accident. A large construction company dump truck driver failed to yield at an intersection where Roosevelt had the right of way. However, once the lawsuit was settled, it was large enough to set Ms. Johnson up for life. Therefore she now teaches for the love of it.

She hopes to one day be that person who provides her students with the spark required in order to change their disruptive course, or ignite those who are on positive courses. As for L.T., she has observed him throughout this year and feels that he has unique qualities unlike any student she's ever taught. Therefore she has decided to challenge L.T.'s determination in regards to getting an education. Upon completion of her talk with the class as a whole Ms. Johnson asks L.T. "Please remain after the bell rings."

He answers "Yes ma'am." Almost as if though on cue the bell signals the end of the day as soon as Ms. Johnson pauses in her speaking. All the students make a mad dash for the door—all except L.T. who remains seated.

Once all the students have left, Ms. Johnson walks over and sits at the desk next to L.T. She then asks, "Why have you spent so much time this year staring out of this window?" Before he answers she says," I've watched you this whole school year sit here and on occasions seemingly stare in the direction of Edison. Again she inquires, "Why son?"

L.T. replies, "Because I've decided to try and attend Edison instead of Frederick Douglas (predominately black and Hispanic)." Ms. Johnson is stunned yet delighted, so much she's almost speechless. But she manages to pull herself together long enough to congratulate L.T. on his intentions. She then asks, "What made you decide to try and enroll at Edison instead of Frederick Douglas?"

L.T. was waiting for this question. He starts from the beginning telling her of his namesakes. L.T. speaks of every detail that pertains to each of them just as they had been told to him. He even speaks of his visits to the library as a result of such heritage. L.T. becomes bright with promise and flushes with emotion as he informs Ms. Johnson of the impact such elements have aided in his maturity. "You see these events resulted in my getting a summer job offer from a Judge Cromwell," he adds.

Now upon learning first hand about what makes L.T. strive, Ms. Johnson is pleased beyond explanation. But it is now time for all students and teachers to leave the school grounds. Therefore Ms. Johnson asks L.T. if he would help her carry some of her material out to her car. L.T. is glad to assist her. So with boxes in hand they exit the building and while walking Ms. Johnson asked L.T. if he'd like to visit her home tomorrow so that she can hear more about his plans. L.T. gladly accepts as they begin putting the items into the car. Afterwards they exchange goodbyes until the next day.

This Friday is the last day of school and L.T. and his classmates are having a good time. They are excited by the usual party, and play different games, while ripping and running in between time. Before the day ends, Ms. Johnson passes out the report cards and even though everyone gets promoted, some have barely managed to make it to the 7th grade. Today's end of the day bell is music to the students' ears. After all the goodbyes everyone seems to vanish into the sunset until next school year. Shortly after all the students are gone L.T. assists Ms. Johnson with the remaining supplies and off to her home they go.

Upon their arrival L.T. is immediately in awe by all the pretty furniture, and the yard, so big. After about forty-five minutes of admiring a black-owned dream home, L.T. manages to get control of himself. Then he and Ms.

Johnson settle down in the formal living room. There they resume discussing L.T.'s future plans and summer job. Ms. Johnson starts their conversation by playing devil's advocate. She asks L.T., "What if the work at Edison middle school is too hard for you—will you dropout and enroll into Frederick Douglas?"

L.T. replies "No way, when I go into that school, no matter what the teachers give me to do, I'll study it until I get it down pat."

Ms. Johnson then inquires, "What if the mostly white kids at Edison don't like you and won't talk to you, what will you do then?"

Without hesitation L.T. answers, "That won't bother me none because I'm a loner. I visit the library alone because I study best alone."

Now after a reasonable amount of time under Ms. Johnson's cross-examination, L.T. proves himself, at least during this conversation, to be a young man with a mission. In the process he has won her support and they both agree that he'll come by to visit from time to time and discuss his progress. Now that they've formed such a solid friendship and due to the fact it's about 7:30 p.m., Ms. Johnson decides to give L.T. a ride home, where she'll be able to meet his parents.

4 *IGNORE NORMALITY*

Transition has always created extra challenges for all individuals who have celebrated more than eighteen birthdays. Having done so, the majority of us have learned firsthand that the meaning of the term hocus-pocus is nonsense words or phrases used as a formula for tricks which are executed only by magicians. Giving consideration to the idea behind following one's dream however, without proper preparation for transition into mainstream society the harsh realities of life aren't magically substituted by your childhood dreams. Furthermore as the passage of time pushes us onward into both adulthood and destiny, our decisions and actions will determine whether we live as a kid who believes in tricks or as an adult who moves forward.

Today is the much anticipated day that L.T. is to meet Judge Cromwell in hopes of landing a job. From the moment he awakes and gets out of bed, his little mind is set on getting this job. Off into the bathroom he goes to execute the daily hygiene routine. L.T. then returns to his room where he gets dressed and packs his bookbag with a few needed materials, two choice library books, along with his end of the year report card. Then it's off to the kitchen for a bowl of Honey Nut Cheerios. Once he's done eating L.T. get his lunch that Thelma prepared last night from the refrigerator and packs it into his trusty bookbag as well. Afterwards he jots down a note just to remind Thelma of his whereabouts and with the aid of a banana shaped magnetic, places it eye-level on the refrigerator's door.

L.T. then swings his bookbag onto his back and puts the note from Judge Cromwell into his front pocket while en route to the metro station. Upon his arrival downstairs into the station terminal, he checks the overhead directory for the blueline scheduled stops to confirm his departure point. Afterwards he purchases a token and goes through the turnstile and boards the train where he picks a window seat. L.T. feels for some unexplainable reason that this particular train ride has a certain aura about it however, he can't quite put his finger on it. Upon the train's arrival at his stop L.T. quickly exits and gets clear of the tracks as he strides briskly towards the stairwell that leads up to the streets. While climbing the steps, he glances at his note once more.

Upon exiting the station terminal L.T. takes a quick look into each direction and in doing so he decides upon his direction of travel in search of Judge Cromwells prestigious neighborhood. Having completed a series of both incorrect and correct turns, he arrives at the plush community wrought iron entrance gate that has a smartly designed guard house positioned out in front. As L.T. walks up to the gate, a tall stocky security guard exits the guard house and inquires, "Are you lost fellow?"

Without uttering a sound L.T. hands him the note from Judge Cromwell. The perplexed guard takes and reads the note and while still in shock he informs L.T., "Wait here I'll have to phone the Judge's resident's." Meanwhile L.T. is all eyes as he tries to sneak a peek through openings within the gate's designs. In doing so L.T. can catch only glimpses of a few of the large and fabulously designed homes.

However, it isn't long before the security guard returns from the guard house and signals for L.T. to come forward which he does. Once L.T. is within earshot, the guard informs him, "The fifth house on the left hand side of the street is the Judge's home," pointing straight down the entrance street. The guard then hands L.T. the note and wishes him good luck. While grabbing the note L.T. walks star gazingly through the gates. While walking and looking from side to side in awe of the architectural marvels that include posted security L.T. forgets to count. To stroll this community makes L.T. feel as if he's dreaming and any minute now his mother is going to wake him up.

Suddenly L.T. arrives in front of what he thinks is the fifth house. Since he hasn't been counting, L.T. looks at his note to check the address on it and then looks up and locates the house address and discovers they match. So with a mixture of uncertainty and excitement, L.T. starts up the long half moon-shaped driveway. Positioned midway up the driveway is a large gray brick home that has a large picture window, its entrance is hidden behind large redwood double doors that are accented with brightly polished brass doorknobs. L.T. gently rings the doorbell and instantly one of the doors open. Much to his surprise, L.T. sees a short black lady who's about his mother's age standing in the doorway. She is dressed in a black maid's uniform with a white collar, white lace sleeves, and she's also wearing a white apron. Her name is Vanessa and she has worked for the Cromwells for nearly twenty years. Vanessa knows from the speechless look upon L.T.'s face that he must be the kid whom the Cromwells are expecting. So she invites him in and closes the door and says, "Please follow me," as she walks toward the patio where the Cromwells are having breakfast.

Once the two of them arrive onto the patio, Vanessa walks over and stands near the serving cart. At which time L.T. introduces himself through a soft trembling voice. Then he nervously walks over and hands the Judge his note which Judge Cromwell takes and reads, chuckling. He then informs his wife Carolyn saying, "Oh yes, honey this is the young heroic gentleman with the ingenious sign I spoke of." Judge Cromwell is a tall dark distinguished-looking gentleman with graying black hair, his neatly trimmed full beard is sprinkled with touches of gray and in some mystic way it illumines his slightly oversized stomach. His charisma and articulate manner of speaking clearly sets the Judge apart from men of his class. He then introduces himself and wife Carolyn.

Carolyn is a brown-skinned woman who stands approximately five feet tall with naturally curly gray hair that has a blue rinse in it. Carolyn also has a pleasantly plump build and a warm sounding voice that instantly makes anyone she meets trust her. Judge Cromwell concludes by introducing Vanessa. Afterwards L.T. shakes everyone's hand. Carolyn then offers him a seat and suggests that he rest from carrying his bookbag. So L.T. spots a patio chair to his right, walks over in front of it, slides his bookbag off, and places it between his legs on the floor as he takes a seat.

Carolyn, in another attempt to break the ice, offers L.T. some breakfast or something to drink. L.T. replies, "Ma'am, I'd like some orange juice please." Vanessa pours a glass of juice and gives it to L.T. who thanks her while grabbing the long-stemmed style glass. In between sips of coffee the

Cromwells ask L.T. a few get-acquainted questions, one being, "How old are you?"

L.T. answers, "I am 12 ma'am."

Carolyn asks, "What grade are you in Luther?"

L.T. replies, "I got promoted to the 7th ma'am." L.T. calmly answers each question adding ma'am and/or sir after each reply. This show of proper mannerism impresses the Cromwells.

However, after about thirty minutes into their conversation L.T. begins to boldly express himself. First he goes into his bookbag and pulls out his report card which he passes to Mrs. Cromwell. Needless to say the A and B honor roll for the entire year impresses the patio's occupants. As a matter of fact it was so impressive to Carolyn she asks L.T., "Are there any other surprises about you that we should know?"

Oh boy! Why did she ask that question? L.T. takes this opportunity to inform her and the Judge about the rich heritage surrounding his name and how learning of such has personally affected him. Talking unlike a child his age from the part of town which he lives, L.T. wins over the Cromwells. Judge Cromwell, who now has L.T.'s report card, examines it again and then pauses for a moment. Afterwards he offers L.T. a job. Both shock and joy collide within L.T.'s thin dark-skinned body resulting in him springing up from his chair much like a rocket during lift-off. L.T. almost could not stop thanking the Cromwells long enough to find out what his hours or pay rate might be or of what chores the job consists. But he does manage to get control of himself when Judge Cromwell asks if three dollars an hour would be enough. To which L.T. replies, "If you are going to pay me three dollars an hour, then I'm going to give you three and a half dollars an hour worth of work."

Judge Cromwell then says, "$3.50 an hour it is."

Both parties then agree that L.T. must work or at least stay at the house for a minimum of four hours a day, from

9:30 a.m. until 1:30 p.m., Monday through Friday with thirty minutes for lunch. He will be paid once a week on Fridays and metro train fare will be paid in addition to his weekly pay. Now in his efforts to assure the Cromwells they have hired a reliable worker, L.T. assures them that he'll never miss a day or be late. So they take his word. The discussion then moves on to the next issue in the negotiation—that being to the understanding that L.T.'s chores are as yet not defined. This is of little importance to L.T. as long as he is hired he is prepared to do whatever it takes to stay employed.

Now that he has gained the Cromwells trust they decide to give L.T. a guided tour of their home, which of course leaves him speechless. Afterwards the understanding is clear that on this coming Monday at 9:30, L.T. will start work. As soon as all of the details are ironed out, the chauffeur Charles comes onto the patio to remind the Judge of his staff meeting. Judge Cromwell introduces Charles and L.T. then assures Charles he'll be ready shortly. L.T. then bids everyone good day and departs to catch the metro train. Upon his arrival back into his own neighborhood L.T., who had been timing himself, discovers that it takes about twenty-five minutes in order to complete the trip one way. As soon as the door slams shut behind him L.T. informs Thelma of his good news. She is so excited and proud of him, she makes it a point to mention it over dinner to the family.

L.T.'s first day of work has come and gone and even his first week has flown past. By and by how time flies. This coming Friday will mark three weeks that L.T. has been working for the Cromwells. Since his hiring L.T. has become very good friends with Vanessa and Tim, the community's day shift security guard whom he met when he first located the community. He and Charles have also become good friends mainly because on Fridays Charles drives him down to the Cromwells' bank in the Judge's limousine to cash his paycheck. Now from the first time

L.T. was driven to the bank while seated in the backseat which Charles suggested he do, L.T. has gotten used to being driven around which has resulted in L.T. wanting his own chauffeur someday. This little morale booster was Carolyn's idea. Every Friday she calls the bank to clear the way for L.T. to cash his check and make a deposit into his saving account as well. A thankful L.T. is well aware of the fact that it isn't a common practice for a twelve-year-old black ghetto boy to be driven around in a stretch limousine that isn't stolen. Needless to say this awesome experience means an awful lot to L.T., then so too has the numerous other small character building ploys the Cromwells have augmented into his routine.

During the past month L.T.'s routine has become established. He is to assist Vanessa for approximately one and a half hours daily, every other day he assists Charles in polishing the Judge's limousine. Then on Thursdays L.T. and Richard, the gardener, take care of the lawn. The aforementioned workload along with a few miscellaneous chores comprises L.T.'s workload. However, these tasks only amount to perhaps three hours daily. Therefore whenever possible L.T. spends time inside the Cromwells library, reading the Judge's law books and other reference material. Upon Carolyn's discovery of L.T.'s quest for knowledge, she okayed his use of the library in his spare time. It should be noted that due to the access to such a vast amount of law material L.T. has decided the type of a career he wants to pursue; that is to become a lawyer. L.T. has always been a kid smarter than his years would indicate. But now that he's surrounded by numerous books which promote structured learning well beyond his years, L.T. is really blooming.

L.T. has worked about half of the summer and today he has decided it's time once again to visit Mrs. Johnson. Upon his arrival Mrs. Johnson is thrilled to know that L.T. is still planning on attending Edison. Mrs. Johnson is just as impressed with how much better structured

L.T.'s conversations have become. His visit today further enhances Mrs. Johnson's admiration for him. Having visited Mrs. Johnson for most of today on this Saturday, L.T. will also pay Mrs. Hepburn a visit later on in the evening. As far as L.T. is concerned, the Schomburg is still the place to do research of any kind. Things haven't changed since his last visit to the library, and Mrs. Hepburn is very pleased to see L.T. once again. The two of them find an unoccupied area to discuss the events of the past month. Much like Ms. Johnson, Mrs. Hepburn can't help but notice the obvious improvement in L.T.'s speech, so much that she informs him of this noticeable change. A shy L.T. can't help showing the shyness that comes with people his age but he does manage to thank Mrs. Hepburn for commenting. However, Mrs. Hepburn then suggests to L.T. that he practice writing in the same manner that he speaks. L.T. assures her that he will practice some penmanship. Then suddenly one of the assistant librarians announces over the PA system the closing announcements. At which time L.T. says, "I guess that's my cue to leave." Afterwards they both share a laugh in agreement before he departs.

Tonight during his usual walk home from the library, L.T.'s mind is busy providing him with pictures of a bright future. This daydreaming takes place in spite of the usual activities happening throughout his neighborhood streets (pimps, prostitution, drug dealing etc...). Driven by such a strong desire to succeed L.T. passes the commotion as if though it is invisible. Momentarily he stops to watch some guys on the basketball courts, but he doesn't feel any urge to try and slam dunk. On the other hand knowing his budget plans are working to perfection really excites him.

With assistance from both the Cromwells and Ms. Johnson, L.T. is striving to duplicate some of the accomplishments of both Dr. King and Booker T. They are getting an education, budgeting, setting and achieving goals are the topics at the forefront of his mind. L.T. knows that since Dr. King and others like him valued these topics, they must be the ingredients for the best kind of life anyone could ever hope to live. Having seen enough basketball he turns away from the fence that encloses four basketball courts and continues his journey home.

As the summer rolls on, L.T. continues to improve in all academic areas. Nightly he practice penmanship, English grammar, and occasionally he even practices speaking in front of mirrors, a technique used to better a person's overall speech. Time and time again, L.T. and Ms. Johnson meet to prepare him for the upcoming school year. During a few of their various meetings, Ms. Johnson plays the devil's advocate by pretending to be a prejudiced teacher and/or a prejudiced kid who doesn't like L.T. and pretends to give L.T. a hard time. All of these games are played in hopes of building L.T.'s character in certain situations. Even though they are just games, Ms. Johnson knows that eventually their preparation will one day come in handy.

Now that summer's about over and school begins again in one week, the Cromwells have decided to allow L.T. to work only on Saturdays so as not to interfere with his schooling. Both parties agree that every Saturday from 9:30 a.m. until 2 p.m. L.T. will work a modified schedule which means that from 9:30 until 12 noon he will do chores and from 12:30 until 2 p.m. he is to study in the library. He will get paid his normal salary of $3.75 an hour for the four and one-half hours plus train fare.

Now that L.T. has survived the long hot dog days of summer, this morning he is up preparing to take on a new challenge. Today is his first day at Edison and L.T. is as nervous—as if it's his first day ever in school. The moment he steps foot onto the school ground, L.T. gets an uneasy feeling but after learning what hour he has what classes and teachers, and his seat assignments, along with a few other first day of school routines, the last bell rings before

L.T. is able to catch his breath. The walk home is a little further than if he'd gone to Frederick Douglas but L.T. doesn't mind because the two neighborhoods he passes through aren't nearly as bad as his own. And it isn't until he gets into his own neighborhood that L.T. gets another eerie feeling and this time rightfully so, because Anthony and his gang have just spotted him. Anthony and his gang members quickly form a circle around L.T. and begin to taunt him.

Anthony questions him asking, "Oh you think you're too good to go to Frederick Douglas, huh?"

L.T. answers, "No its just that the courses offered at Frederick Douglas are not as helpful in growth and development as those offered at Edison." L.T. adds, "Besides the materials and faculties are some of the best in the state at Edison."

Following on the heels of L.T.'s reply, one of the gang members asks him, "You think that by you going to Edison with their better materials as you say, is going to make them white students and teachers look at you any different than they look at us?"

Before L.T. could respond another gang member states, "No matter what you fool yourself into believing you're still a product of the ghetto."

L.T. turns to face the one member who questioned him first, stares him in the eye and says, "Perhaps at first their opinion might be to think that I can't hang but once I'm given the opportunity to prove that I'm capable of completing any assignment given, then yes, they will change their opinion of me." He then faces the second member and replies," I'm well aware of the fact that whatever I accomplish my achievements will be attributed to a one time ghetto citizenship."

Now those answers by L.T. were the best thing he could have come up with at that particular moment because it made the whole gang laugh so hard and long until they all simply laughed themselves away from him. But L.T.

wasn't phased at all as he continued on home. Then he went to the library as usual.

Now on this the second day of classes during fifth period it dawns on L.T. that each of his teachers today has made a comment about his enrollment which is unlikely due to his address. Due to the school's location, not many blacks ever attempt to attend, even forced bussing hasn't been able to generate noticeable integration. The sound of today's final bell is music to L.T.'s ears.

As L.T. starts out on his walk home, a group of white kids follow him instigating along the way, until suddenly the kid L.T. allowed to copy from his pop science quiz shows up. Geno is his name and he happens to be the Italian kid who's nickname is "Hitman." Geno's goal is to someday become a professional hitman. As he puts it, "Not just any hitman, but the one people request only for special occasions." Needless to say once Geno comes onto the scene all the other kids quickly scatter. Then he and L.T. began talking about the activities of today, and some of the things that go on at the school, and about the cool kids and those to be leery of as well. During the course of their conversation and while walking they must pass Geno's home where Geno invites L.T. to stop and visit for a minute.

Once inside Geno's room L.T. sees all of these guns (real guns) and they prompt him to inquire, "Who owns all of these?"

Shock grips his very soul when Geno answers, "Me," without any indication of a joke. Geno begins showing off the many varieties he has; hand guns, automatics, and even a high-powered 30-06 rifle equipped with a state-of-the-art scope, which Geno states is his favorite. All of these weapons have shaken L.T. who informs Geno that he must leave quickly. Geno understands so he shows him to the door where they exchange farewells.

A distraught L.T. soon discovers that todays trials aren't over yet as he observes Lazerbeam in his path. He seem to have appeared out of nowhere. Lazerbeam judges from L.T.'s sulking appearance that he's running into problems at Edison and therefore Lazerbeam decides to take this opportunity to try and score. Lazerbeam attempts to ease his way into L.T.'s grace as he inquires, "Say Little Einstein, the white folks testing your character?"

L.T., aware of the fact that he's having a bad day, decides he need not let it be a good day recruiting-wise for Lazerbeam. Therefore, he pulls himself together and answers Lazerbeam saying, "Life is full of peaks and valleys, I'll be okay."

Lazerbeam then comments, "Say Little Einstein don't you forget I'm the one who can make your life full of nothing but peaks."

A steadily moving L.T. doesn't even bother to give a response to that comment, as he continues walking on home.

Once home L.T. is in and out quicker than usual and he's off to Ms. Johnson's place, where he arrives shortly after she does. There the two of them begin a discussion about today's events. Afterwards much to Ms. Johnson's delight, she is proud to see that such trying activities have served to motivate L.T. instead of discourage him. Ms. Johnson mostly serves as an ear for L.T. to vent his frustrations, occasionally offering a suggestion or two. Again Ms. Johnson is surprised at how often L.T. mentions her efforts over the summer when she was attempting to prepare him for just such happenings. Once he is through venting his frustrations and being reassured of his capabilities, L.T. bids her good night and departs.

It has been nearly a month since L.T.'s teachers discreetly challenged his decision to attend Edison. However, his faith within himself has again provided L.T. with the answer to yet another questionable situation within his life. This is evident in that L.T.'s lowest average is 93% in science. Two weeks before report cards are due L.T. is confident that his efforts and study habits can produce his desired results under any circumstances.

At this timeframe in L.T.'s life he has nothing but positive expectations.

Then just as a number of things in life are subject to change without notice, so too does Lazerbeam's appearance. Lazerbeam observes a vibrant L.T. returning from the library therefore Lazerbeam tries to add fuel to L.T.'s enthusiasm. A confident Lazerbeam strikes a cross-legged pose against his silver and black BMW and as L.T. approaches within ear shot he asks, "Say Little Einstein do you want to take a cruise around the borough in my Beamer?" L.T. takes a good hard look at this fine automobile all the while taking in the slick designs and tinted windows—it even has a phone and for a moment he almost answers yeah.

But a stern, "No" bursts through his lips! Even though he doesn't have control of his actions, L.T. discovers himself walking away from Lazerbeam.

A stunned Lazerbeam walks up behind L.T. and grabs a hold of his loaded bookbag then asks, "Don't you know the reputation associated with driving a Beamer?" He adds, "A BMW means success!"

L.T. then informs Lazerbeam, "If you live in a Harlem ghetto and drive a BMW, it only means one thing—Black Men Won't—succeed that is." L.T. adds, "On the other hand if a Beamer is the automobile that can be purchased within a well-structured budget, which includes a mortgage, provided wholesome employment is what fuels your budget, then BMW stands for Best Methods Work."

Having heard enough Lazerbeam replies, "That's cold Einstein, cold but deep too." A retreating Lazerbeam continues shaking his head from side to side indicating defeat while strolling on back towards his BMW. Meanwhile L.T. simply continues on his way home.

5 *SIMMERING POTENTIAL*

Citizens of this world must realize you can't blame the entire population for an act, any more than you can blame a whole race for some members of a group. The smoldering suggestions compiled within these pages were written with the hope that numerous noteworthy yet unidentifiable individuals might be epitomized. The unidentifiable individuals I'm referring to are the numerous African forefathers and their American offspring whose legendary characteristics and contributions may forever be an integral part of America's society. The audacity of the previously mentioned pioneers provides America with a subliminal aura.

However, for centuries shortly after any trailblazer succumbs to death, numerous frightening and unfortunate trends unfold at alarming rates in this country. For most African-Americans, their existence in their birth land has been like a leaking resolution. Place a solution under one problem and there springs three more dilemmas within the same area. Even though African-Americans have climbed the ladder of life rung by rung, such feats still have not allowed them the opportunity to feel the warmth of the nation's consciousness. Needless to mention the outlook is dark, but hopefully commitment to equitable existence will provide the world's ultimate untapped resources, African Americans, an opportunity to witness the shining light of a new day.

In spite of the sensitivity involved with the completion of such a task, dialogue alone isn't enough. The often quoted phrases like, "Freedom, Justice and Equality," require a lifelong journey, not a brief trip, and do not provide adequate evidence to justify the use of unwarranted discrimination.

Just as sure as the hot summer season gives way to the wet autumn and winter follows them both, such continuing process results in the passing of years. Three very enlightening years have passed since L.T. was hired by the Cromwells. L.T. has kept his word in regards to not missing a day or being late, and the Cromwells have rewarded him with four raises. L.T. is now about to enter high school, well the 9th grade to be exact, and the Cromwells have decided to let him in on their little secret that pertains to him. On this Saturday morning, which happens to be the last weekend of summer, the Cromwells are seated on their patio over breakfast. Vanessa and Charles are also present.

Suddenly the Judge takes his spoon and begins tapping the side of his glass in the manner of getting everyone's attention. "Attention everyone! Carolyn and I have an announcement to make." All eyes are on him now as he nods to Carolyn at which time she picks up a bank book.

Carolyn and Judge Cromwell then stand up and Carolyn announces, "At this time we would like L.T. to know that this is an eight thousand dollar Trust Fund Account which was opened three years ago with the hope that he will continue to strive as he has." She continues, "And should he continue to maintain the effort and progress he has shown in these first three years while working for us in his next four, then upon graduation this Trust Fund will be awarded to him."

Judge Cromwell adds, "I second that motion!"

A surprised L.T. just couldn't hold back his tears of joy. Vanessa comes to his rescue by wrapping her arms around him while informing L.T., "I know how you feel believe me I do." She adds, "When you live in our neighborhood and something like this happens in your life, its a blessing from God almighty." Between Vanessa's comforting words L.T. regains his composure long enough to thank the Cromwells for making his dream of attending college possible. He assures all of the patio occupants that his attitude and effort will not change.

Judge Cromwell quickly ask L.T., "What will you major in college?"

L.T. respectfully snaps, "Law. I'd like to be a lawyer so that maybe I can help those who need defending the most."

At which time the Judge states, "Why stop at lawyer? Hell you're as good a judge as I am." Everyone then follows the Judge's lead in laughter. Due to this decision the Cromwells have indicated that they've chosen L.T. to fill the void in their lives from lack of having children. Carolyn suffered through two traumatic miscarriages and after the second she and Ed decided against trying anymore. They entertained ideas for awhile about adopting but agreed that they both were too selfish to share one another with children anyway. Upon completion of this very moving and informative session, L.T. departs to tell his family of the good news, while the Cromwells continue to prepare for their vacation to Japan.

A jubilant L.T. can't wait to inform his parents of the event of his life. But once he exits from the metro station, he and others are subjected to a violent and disturbing scene. There is a gang of about five guys with guns and knives who have virtually beaten and cut Geno within an inch of his life. Off to the side near the street curb lays Geno's M-16 with the magazine loaded. As L.T. observes in shock he overhears the leader taunting Geno as he and other gang members stomp and kick Geno about his body from head to toe. The gang isn't from Geno's borough but their leader tells Geno, "If you come over into our borough and shoot-up our turf then we are going to find your ass anywhere in this city and do the same shit to you."

By this time sirens could be heard seemingly on every corner and suddenly the gang leader signals for his members to stop. As they turn and begin walking away, still holding their weapons in their hands, two gang members turn and aim their weapons at Geno's blood drenched body when suddenly M-16 automatic fire dances all around them! Naturally this unexpected action made them scatter! As the gang disappears a shocked driven L.T. runs up to Geno's battered body kneels and shouts, "Geno it's me, L.T. Don't die, I'll dump your gun." L.T. then breaks out running through the alley way with the M-16 in his righthand which he dropped in the first dumpster he passes.

Now some distance from the scene, his heart pounding so pronounced it feels as if though it will leave his chest, L.T. tries to regain his composure. Once he has regrouped L.T. discovers that during his daring moment of glory he ran farther away from home instead of closer. So he cautiously turns and heads in the direction of home when after a couple of blocks, he runs into none other than Anthony and his gang. However this approach towards L.T. is noticeably different from the previous ones, because they've witnessed L.T. in action as Anthony states it. Without further ado Anthony informs L.T. that at this time he will join them or else he will personally inform that gang of not only his identity, but also he'll personally show them where L.T. lives. At this particular moment L.T. begins to brainstorm, knowing that he must think of a plan fast. Wham! He's got it, but he must run it through his mind's thought process very carefully first. So he puts on a macho act in order to buy himself some more time. L.T. begins by staring each member up and down as a indication of thinking, slowly moving his eyes from each member's feet to his head, then momentarily stares into their eyes before moving to the next guy and repeating his actions. L.T.'s outward appearance is that of a future gang member while inwardly his mind is being battered about like storm driving waves against the seashore. The sounds of Albert's voice on that night he stressed blacks must shatter these types of myths echoes throughout L.T.'s soul.

Without farther hesitation L.T. agrees to join but with conditions—those conditions are they have to prove themselves to him not he prove himself to them. Another condition is if he doesn't have school work to do then he runs with them, but only in his spare time. And last but not least, he won't spearhead committing any crimes but will only serve as backup. Now that L.T. has made his conditions known to the gang, the members step away from L.T.'s earshot where they form a circle in order to discuss and vote on L.T.'s conditional membership. As L.T. observes the gang members discussing his status, L.T.'s true feelings bubble inside of him. At that moment his uncertainties team up with his conscious.

The truth be known, L.T. never wanted any of the events of the past hour to ever have a place in his life. And joining this or any gang has always been totally out of the question, but Geno did save him from numerous fights over the years and besides it really wasn't him that fired that gun it was actually fear that pulled the trigger. And of all the people in Harlem to witnessing his heroic deed provided Anthony and his gang with the ammunition needed to force L.T. to join them. But even so he thought that he could bluff his way for a little while longer, or at least buy himself some time from these guys. Even now as he watches them over there discussing his fate, L.T. doesn't know what to expect. Just like his intentions weren't to go all the way with these guys, perhaps they are thinking the same about him.

On top of all this mystery, who's to say one of those guys won't get upset at him one day and still sell him out to that gang. The longer he analyzes his dilemma the more uneasy L.T. becomes, and on top of it all, this happens on what had seemed to be the happiest day of his life. The members are now walking back towards him when Anthony pauses for a moment and tells L.T. his membership will have be put on hold, but the conditions part of it is out of the question. Anthony then informs L.T. that he's got one week to come all the way or else he can't promise L.T. anything. After that statement he and his members walk away leaving L.T. feeling confused. At this particular moment L.T. is uncertain if he has dodged a bullet. Nonetheless a perplexed L.T. continues home.

Once home a dejected L.T. puts on a happy face as he still manages to tell of the Cromwells plan which will greatly enhance his chance to attend college. Thelma and Albert burst into tears as they feel an overwhelming sense of pride. Throughout the night everyone relishes the idea of L.T. attending college.

On this particular Sunday morning, preparation for church takes on a new meaning for an uneasy L.T. They arrive at church and find a whole bench which is required in order to seat the entire Thompson family. Shortly after they're seated services began. Midway through the order of service, the choir sings a beautiful number, *Jesus is a Miracle worker*, from their hymn books. Now the time has come for Reverend T. L. Brown to preach his sermon. As Rev. Brown starts his way up to the podium he begins singing the song "Oh Happy Day," in the old Negro tradition. Naturally the choir backs him up and the church members join in: "Oh happy day—When I get to heaven—oh happy day, I'm going to sing and shout!"

Perhaps due to his underlining troubles today this song strikes a chord within L.T. so much that he stands and joins Thelma and a number of other ladies within the congregation singing and clapping with a purpose.

After approximately three to four minutes Rev. Brown raises his hands to calm the congregation. Following a few administrative announcements, the pastor informs the church that the title of his sermon today consists of just one word—Faith. He then states, "For those of you who have your Bibles with you, my text comes from Hebrews 11:1-8 verses." Rev. Brown continues saying, "This particular chapter is known to all who are truly Christians." He then urges the church to read along with him as he reads the first verse aloud, "'Now faith is the substance of things hoped for, the evidence of things not seen.'" Rev. Brown then gives the congregation a few examples of what this verse means in the lives of true Christians.

He begins by saying in the biblical days people faced the same type of problems we face today. For example it was by faith that Abel won out over his brother Cain even though Abel was dead. There is also the story in the Bible of a woman who was sick it could even be said that she had AIDS, but by her faith she was healed when she simply touched the hem of Jesus robe. Her faith was so strong that when she touched the hem of Jesus' robe, even though there was a multitude of people, Jesus felt this woman's touch. Rev. Brown is now well into his sermon and it seems to L.T. as if each word is spoken for his sake. During his efforts to bring on home his sermon's message Rev. Brown continues in that old Negro preaching tradition saying, "If there is anyone in here today facing any kind of a problem or hurdle in your life, brothers and sisters if you'll just put your faith in God Almighty, you might not know it yet—but that hurdle is already behind you!" He concludes by saying, "In time and through faith, you will come to know as I've told you so.'

Hearing such a moving sermon leads L.T. to really think about the faith he has within himself, so much that he will talk with his mother the first chance he gets so that he might come to feel as strongly about achieving his life's goals as Pastor Brown spoke of today. It is customary for the pastor to walk down the center aisle prior to releasing the congregation, so that he will be in a position to exchange greetings with departing patrons. Today L.T. feels compelled to shake the pastor's hand before leaving because due to today's sermon he feels good about himself and feels he owes it to Rev Brown.

The following Monday afternoon L.T. is able to get Thelma's attention for a talk he feels he desperately needs. During his attempt to gain her attention, she is as cordial as always. Now is as good a time as any since Albert has taken Pam and Toby to register for the upcoming school term. As L.T. asks one question after another Thelma patiently answers each as thoroughly and straightforward as she can. Sometimes she even gives him an example in an attempt to clarify her point. Once it has become obvious to Thelma that L.T. has about run out of questions, she feels it appropriate to praise him and let him know how proud she is of him. Naturally he begins to blush.

But then Thelma turns the conversation to a more serious tone when she indicates that she wants L.T. to promise her something. To which he replies, "Of course Mama, anything." Thelma then states, "I want you to promise me that for the rest of your natural life you'll always practice the teaching of four particular places."

L.T. is quick to inquire, "What are the four places mama?"

She answers, "They are the church, bank, library, and the gym." Thelma quickly adds, "I know you're already familiar with church and its teachings as well as the library, and bank's too." She now attempts to choose her words as she speaks softly saying, "Son I know you don't play any sports and I'm not asking you to start now, but honey, you should go to the gym and work out your body by exercising or swimming, okay."

L.T. assures her that he will keep that promise and use those places for all their worth. Before concluding Thelma decides to share her feeling with L.T. pertaining to his dream(s) of attending college and achieving all of his life's goals. She says, "Son I would love nothing better than to see all of your dreams in life come true." Thelma pauses then states, "But there's another point about life you must never forget and that pertinent point is this— dreams can't compare to goals already achieved."

Just as Thelma completes saying this noted phrase L.T. shouts, "Mama that's deep. I'm going to adopt that as my life's motto." A motivated L.T. then repeats the phrase once more before bursting out of the kitchen and into his room where he writes it down.

No change ever takes place without conflict. This statement is certainly the truth anytime Lazerbeam and L.T. confront one another. The only problem is one has to be more committed to standing on the truth than the other. Tonight L.T. is strolling around the borough just trying to sort out some of the issues that have bombarded him lately. Almost out of nowhere Lazerbeam slowly drives up behind him in his BMW and lowers the passenger side window and says to L.T., "Get in."

L.T. asks, "What make you think that I'm going to ever fall for one of your little pranks?"

Lazerbeam replies, "Because tonight I want to show you that the gang members who you thought might one day come after you are dead."

As he walks a semi-interested L.T. asks, "Are you talking about the gang that roughed up Geno?"

Lazerbeam shouts, "Yea man I'm talking about them thugs. They just got smoked across town and I wanted you to look into their dead faces for yourself. Because by looking into their dead faces you'll know." Lazerbeam adds, "Out here on these streets no man is taken at 'only' his word—his word backed-up with action is what develops his reputation."

After such a strong lesson in gaining a reputation on the streets by Lazerbeam, L.T. stops in his tracks. He then walks up and leans over onto Lazerbeam's passenger side window where L.T. looks Lazerbeam directly into his eyes and says, "It is unfortunate that black brothers like yourself read phrases like the one that states NO CHANGE EVER TAKES PLACE WITHOUT CONFLICT all the wrong way." L.T. then says, "Thanks for the information about the gang. It certainly eased my mind." He then steps away from the car and continues his evening stroll. Lazerbeam speeds off into the night!

A numb L.T. practically lost the past two days of his life as he tries to put into proper perspective the blowing winds of change. Nevertheless a relieved L.T. decides to visit Ms. Johnson in hopes that she might help him to return his focus back onto school. It seems as if Ms. Johnson had read L.T.'s mind. Shortly after his arrival, she dives right into wholesome educational conversation. Ms. Johnson knows that tonight L.T. must be made aware of some serious information. Therefore she starts by questioning him about the importance of ninth grade classes and grades serving as prerequisite for attending college. Ms. Johnson informs him the ninth through the twelfth grades represent the timeframe when various grades and test results are reviewed by colleges in order to determine a student's acceptance. A spellbound L.T. softly states, "I didn't know that."

Ms. Johnson then cautions him that the choice of classes a student takes is also important beginning at the ninth grade level. She then asks to see a list of L.T.'s upcoming classes. L.T. gathers up a pen and a note pad and writes out his classes in order which reads:

Level 4 - Algebra - 1st hour

Level 4 - U.S. History -2nd hour

Level 4 - Freshman Composition - 3rd hour

Level 4 - Biology - 4th hour

Physical Education - 5th hour

Art (Painting & drawing) - 6th hour

After reviewing the list Ms. Johnson informs L.T. that he has made excellent choices. She then turns the discussion to the topic of homework by saying, "As far as I can tell, you complete your homework in a timely and accurate manner." Ms. Johnson then forcefully states, "From this year forward it's a must that your homework is completed in such a manner that it literally speaks for you." Afterwards she pointedly questions, "Do you understand me?"

A stunned L.T. answers with a positive, "Yes ma'am!" L.T. can't help but notice the sternness within Ms. Johnson's actions and conversation tonight, so he comments about her actions.

Ms. Johnson answers him straightforward saying, "There is a scholarship program offered every year throughout this state to high school seniors and by the time you're a senior I want you to win this contest." She adds, "But I don't want you to win it for me, or put forth the effort because I think it's the thing to do. I want you to challenge this contest for yourself." Ms. Johnson continues, "I believe that you are capable of winning, but the most important thing is how you feel." Then in a sharp tone she inquires, "Does that answer your question?" Immediately after her emotional outburst she apologizes to him for seeming so short.

L.T. assures her that he is grateful for this information and again assures her that he'll do all he can in order to win that scholarship because it is his future at stake. The two of them then break into smiles and the tension erases. Upon observing the clock which reads nine p.m. Ms. Johnson states, "I'd better give you a ride home so that you'll live long enough to compete." That comment brings a laugh from the both of them.

The days following that discussion seem to intensify L.T.'s focus and determination. Coupled with knowing that the blackmailing evidence Anthony's gang once held no longer exists propels him to new heights. He and Thelma shop for school clothes and supplies as if though it is a military mission instead of just the start of another school year.

Once school starts L.T.'s bedtime changes from nine to closer to ten thirty due to his studying habits. He uses only twenty minutes daily to eat his sack lunch and uses the remaining forty minutes to review the morning classes. Saturdays are used for working and studying at the Cromwells, exercising or swimming at the YMCA, and occasionally a movie. Now in this the second grade period of the school year, the myth about L.T.'s inability to play any team sport has become a noticeable fact. Now this myth becomes fact because many of the kids noticed that during physical education class any time they square off to choose teams, L.T. disappears to workout in the exercise room.

However, being black L.T. can't avoid being asked to play a team sport forever. So one week his classmates corner him and choose him to play basketball for a few days. In that short span L.T. erases the myth and makes it fact that he can't play basketball or football either. The results hold true for baseball as well. Naturally this stumbling block troubles L.T. in that it might effect his P.E. grade. Therefore he decides to visit Coach Washington and questions him as to whether his inability to play a team sport will noticeably affect his grade, even though he participates to the best of his ability.

Coach Washington calls every kid "brother" be he black, white or otherwise. Questioned by L.T., Coach replies, "L.T., you are a unique brother I must admit, I've never ever seen a black ghetto-born and raised brother who couldn't play one team sport, until I met you." Coach then adds, "But then when I see you working out in the exercise room you seem as if you're trying to become another Bo Jackson or somebody. And for that reason alone you're an A-number one guy with me." Now that reply does more for L.T.'s heart than Cupid's arrow ever will, and needless to say it allows him to function again. L.T. turns and begins heading for the showers when Coach Washington yells out to him, "Hey L.T. brother, you stay into them books you hear, because there's enough of us already chasing after them different balls."

6 *SUCCESS ISN'T A MATTER OF CHOICE*

No matter what their intentions, people can't change their course of destiny. Time changes circumstances. What's up one day can be down the next. However we can be assured the cards of life will switch hands and so the table of balance rearranges. Therefore, no one knows if his life's existence will be one that is dominated by bouts of temporary temptation or one that will ooze permanent joy. Today marks the completion of L.T.'s second year as a qualified candidate for the scholarship contest and promotion to the eleventh grade. It's still much too early to tell of his standings among the other contestants.

Summertime means full-time work at the Cromwells as a part of L.T.'s routine. L.T. also feels he must check in with Ms. Johnson periodically, because at this time she is his educational navigator. Ms. Johnson is doing all she can to insure that each day is planned in such a manner that it provides L.T. with maximum growth. Thanks to the Cromwells and Ms. Johnson, L.T. has placed such huge expectations upon himself and to choose between success and failure, isn't a matter of choice at all.

L.T. has become an avid jogger. Daily in any type of weather he jogs about three miles, either at the YMCA or outdoors. Without remorse the almost unbearable hot summer days continue to click off and within every passing hour the mixture of howling sirens and gunfire can be heard around the clock. Now on this particular Saturday evening as L.T. is about to complete his daily jog, he turns the corner for the stretch leg home, when suddenly he hears machine gun fire. Everyone who lives in this neighborhood is accustomed to gun fights, but today's gun fire seems to have a name written on it. Naturally L.T. becomes curious as he observes the crowd gathering at the scene of the shooting. His curiosity quickly changes to shock once close enough to identify four of the five victims. Anthony Bates and three of his gang members along with a 13-year-old girl lie scattered about the sidewalk and street.

L.T. and the others then hear one of the witness say that the shooting had taken place all because of that guy (pointing to Anthony). He had made it a habit of taking the gunman's baby brother's money. The witness added, "So today Robert (the gunman) gave his little brother five dollars because he had gone to the library all week and read three books." He continues, "So naturally once little Tim received the money he headed for the corner store to buy himself some ice cream, but before Tim could get to the store that bully and his three sidekicks took his money. But today Robert was watching the whole thing from underneath that fire escape, so he called Tim over to his side then when his brother got beside him, he pulled his Uzi from behind his back and open fire. I'm sure he didn't mean to kill the girl but she was in the line of fire. That's a part of life in the ghetto," he concludes.

Afterwards L.T. takes a closer look at Anthony's bullet-riddled body and notices two things in particular. First of all a bullet had hit smack between his eyes and secondly a five dollar bill was clenched tightly in his left hand. Before L.T. leaves the scene, the innocent girl's mother comes running and falls over the top of her daughter's lifeless body, crying her eyes out. Between the mother's tears, L.T. is able to make out her disheartened words which she screamed, "O Lord, why? My baby was a straight A student, my baby is gone. Oh Lord I'll never get out of this place." Understanding the nature of this woman's pain brings tears to L.T.'s eyes as he runs away from the scene.

A sorrowful L.T. thinks about attending the funeral services of the victims; he feels compelled to attend the funeral of the straight A student. Upon his arrival at the church he finds it full to capacity and throughout the service school officials praise the girl's accomplishments and mourn the loss of such potential. Learning of the achievements she had already achieved make this funeral the hardest one L.T. had attended in his life. While observing the body being driven away to its final resting place, the reality behind the lack of effort of numerous blacks to stop potential genocide among themselves hits him like a ton of bricks. The mere sight of that hearse injects more pain into L.T.'s heart than any bullet ever could.

During his walk home L.T. passes the church where Anthony's funeral is being held and notices that his family was the majority in attendance. Once off the busy streets and now alone with his thoughts, L.T. can't help but reflect back to the days when Anthony and those same three guys would corner him in attempts to make him join their gang. But then he also can't resist thinking about that little straight A student whose life appeared to have been so promising but was cut down by a nobody whose life was destined to end as it did. Momentarily L.T. feels firsthand the meaning of the phrase, "A person's actions don't only affect that one individual alone, they always affect someone else as well."

Now it is often said that time has a way of healing all wounds and over the remaining course of the summer L.T. is able to live with the events of the past. In time an ironic twist of fate spares L.T. from one form of temptation that often leads to destruction. Walking on a fine line through his life's maze, L.T. withstands most of the setbacks he has encountered thus far really well. Many events of this particular summer again have L.T. looking forward to the start of school once more. However prior to the start of school he and Thelma shop with a purpose while choosing clothes and supplies. L.T. relishes the idea of another year of stiff competition.

This glimpse at his report card after the first semester indicates L.T.'s potential for being competitive throughout the contest. His report card reads:

Classes:	Grade/Semester Avg:
Chemistry	A-4.0
French I	A-4.0
Speech I	A-4.0
(English course in Public Speaking)	
Algebra II	A-4.0
Economics	A-4.0
(Emphasis on micro-economics)	
Business Computers I	A-4.0

As the school year passes L.T. maintains the same grade point average throughout the year. However, so do

two other candidates. At the completion of his junior year
L.T. begins to feel a lot like the woman Reverend Brown
preached about (If she could only touch the hem of Jesus
garment, she knew she'd be saved). L.T. feels that as long
as his efforts match his faith then together there is no way
God would deny him victory.

The steamy days of summer have rolled around once
again bringing with them intensified sounds of the city
and death in many forms. This summer one of L.T.'s main
concerns is to live through it so that hopefully he'll be able
to realize his dream of attending college. More and more
while studying he has had to drop to the floor due to gun
fire that enters and ricochets around their home. Ms.
Johnson and the Cromwells have offered L.T. the opportunity to live with them until graduation and Thelma and
Albert have left the decision up to him, but he chooses to
live with his parents.

Meanwhile as a determined L.T. looks forward to traveling an unfamiliar road into the future Jason is certain
of the mode and course of travel into his future. Jason
has fully committed himself to the Nation if Islam and
has also decided to move to Chicago. The news of Jason's
decision is bittersweet to Albert and Thelma. However
they are both proud of him but sad that he has decided
to move away. Jason continues to disclose his previous
decisions by informing his parents that he has dropped
his slave name and from now on will be known as
Muhammad Shabazz. Now that statement prompts
Thelma to inquire, "You've really committed yourself
haven't you?" Before Muhammad could reply she adds,
"After all of those years of preaching to you about the
type of company you were keeping, I never thought something like this would result from those times. All of the
Muslims I've ever seen are really well-mannered,"
Thelma concludes.

Muhammad Shabazz then states, "Mama, the Muslim
faith is designed in such a manner whereby anyone who

wishes to help themselves can do so once shown the right teachings." He adds, "Anytime someone is surrounded by people who have successfully overcome problems and indecision that another is presently facing, and if proven techniques are applied, in both cases similar results are almost certain."

Albert speaks saying, "Son, I want you to know that I'm proud of you for this decision that you've made at such a critical point in your life." Albert adds, "I feel that you've reached the crossroads within your life." He continues, "When a man reaches a certain point in life where he's outgrown the things he used to do, but is unsure of himself and what it is he wants to do, nonetheless he still must do something." Tears slowly fills Albert's eyes as he states, "Now your mother and I didn't have a choice between this ghetto and some Long Island residential community. However, even though you all were raised in such a bad surroundings I'm glad to say that so far the tentacles of destruction haven't been able to snatch either of you from life's wholesome path. Thelma and I would love to see each of you leave this ghetto on as positive note as you are. Congratulations, son, and may Allah forever be with you," Albert concludes.

Muhammad then takes a long look at his folks and seeing tears filling up in the wells of their eyes decides to tell a joke instead of mentioning his departure which breaks the sadness felt by everyone. However, after the laughter subsides Muhammad informs them that in four days, which will be Saturday, he'll be leaving on the bus.

Two days later a jubilant Albert comes home from work and bursts into the house calling for Thelma at the top of his voice, so it seemed to her. Thelma runs into the living room answering, more appropriately asking, "Albert, honey, what is it? What's happened? Is something wrong?"

He then challenges Thelma asking, "Guess what?"

Thelma's in no mood to guess and replies, "I can't guess. You tell me."

Albert informs her, "I'm one of the finalists for district representative of the union!" He continues saying, "Tom Johnson and Willie Burton told me after I clocked in, but I didn't believe those jokers. Then around 10 o'clock I was called into the office and told by the administrators that I am indeed one of the two finalists."

Albert adds, "You see honey ,the union will announce the winner in about nine months once Fred Williamson, the present representative retires." Continuing he says, "To be district representative is to be the voice for nearly five thousand union members."

Thelma, now as excited as Albert, exclaims, "That's wonderful sweetheart, I'm sure you'll win." Throughout the Thompson's household only good things are happening or on the verge of happening, so it seems. Through it all Thelma is the one person most sought after to be informed first, or better yet, it is her opinion and approval everyone seeks.

On the other hand Sara has been disappearing most of the week, and all day Friday, the day prior to Muhammad's date to leave. Naturally Sara's behavior makes Thelma uneasy. Being the concerned mother that she is, Thelma wakes up early on Saturday morning and goes into Sara and Pam's bedroom where she hopes to talk with Sara before Muhammad leaves, in case his leaving has anything to do with Sara's mood swing. But to Thelma's surprise when she eases open the door to the girls bedroom, Sara is already wide awake sitting up in bed writing a letter to Debra. Debra, a former member of Sara's so-called posse, is now in the state prison. Sara is informing Debra of her decision to enter the Air Force as a journalist.

Thelma is unaware of Sara's decision so she immediately questions her asking, "What's the matter baby? Does Jason's leaving New York have anything to do with you feeling sad these last couple of days?"

Sara answers, "No, not really, Mama. I'm happy to see him branch out and grow." She adds sadly, "In a way." Sara then states, "But from talking with Jason, I mean Muhammad, and hearing what he has to say about his decision and knowing how the situation is supposed to be when he arrives in Chicago, I'm happier than I am sad." She then questions Thelma, "Why do you ask?"

Thelma replies, "Well this whole week it seems as if though you was sad, and yesterday I didn't hardly see you at all."

Sara senses that now is the time to inform Thelma about her decision, so she starts by saying, "Mama, I've decided that it's time I make some hard decisions in my life also, just as Muhammad has done." She adds, "Muhammad and I talked about different things, mostly about growing up and leaving Harlem. We also recalled how you and daddy have fought to raise five kids in this three bedroom rowhouse." Sara quickly adds, "Now don't get me wrong. We both are aware that it wasn't due to your's and daddy's choosing that you two raised us in this type of neighborhood but due to a few unfortunate setbacks that led to daddy not being able to earn the kind of money needed in order to live in the suburbs. So I've decided to make a change in my life also. Yesterday I joined the Air Force," Sara adds. Naturally Sara's show of independence surprises Thelma but it also makes her proud as well.

They continue their conversation as they walk into the kitchen and while preparing breakfast for the family. Once everyone is seated and eating, Thelma suddenly speaks up so that she might get everyone's attention, which she does. A teary-eyed Thelma softly says, "Today is one of the saddest days of my life, but then it's one of the happiest too." She turns to look Muhammad in his eyes and says, "Son, I just want you to know that no matter where you go, or what you do with your life I'll always be here for you." Thelma then turns to Sara and assures her of the same. Shortly after assuring Sara that the door is always open, Thelma announces to the family Sara's decision to join the Air Force.

Afterwards L.T. shouts his approval stating, "Alright Sis! Go on with your bad self!" He then states, "Fill us in on all the details of your master plan."

Sara speaks, "I just want everyone to know that yesterday I enlisted into the Air Force to become a journalist. But I don't leave until next month."

L.T. leads the family's applauds. Albert carefully fights back tears of joy as he too claps his hands. Muhammad then speaks, "I just want to say to my family, even though our residence is the ghetto we couldn't ask for more than what we've already received—living as a unit with both our parents still together and all of us still alive along with having love and unity." He continues, "Those facts alone make us better off than many rich families because usually where ever money is present, so too is jealousy. I'm proud to be a member of this family." Muhammad adds, "Because I know from the bottom of my heart that if at anytime for any reason, if any of us might need another's help, all we'll have to do is ask." He concludes saying, "I love every one of you more than I love myself."

Now after such a moving speech both Albert and L.T. have to choke back tears. Both manage to do so before L.T. leads applause for Muhammad. The time has come for Muhammad to leave. While Albert and Thelma wait in the car Muhammad says his goodbyes to all his younger sisters and brothers. Now as he hugs and shakes L.T.'s hand he asks, "Well little brother, do you have any words of wisdom for your big brother?"

L.T. replies, "Yes as a matter of fact I do," while pointing his right index finger toward Muhammad in a scolding manner, "Your attitude is what describes to you what you want to be. It just may not be what the people see."

Muhammad then replies, "I like that, matter of fact, I'm going to adopt it as my life's motto." He then hugs L.T. one last time and runs out and gets into the car and Albert drives off.

One short month later the family is bidding Sara farewell. Since she is scheduled to leave on Monday and school is in session, the family decides to have their little get-together and speeches during Sunday dinner after church. Sara's final night flies by and today her flight leaves at eight a.m. Even though she is up and out of bed at five a.m. Sara comes upon L.T. in the kitchen studying for a test. There she and L.T. begin a discussion about parables of life. Suddenly Sara confides in L.T. when she states, "I'm unsure if I can stand up to the challenge ahead of me."

Upon hearing her L.T. looks Sara square into her eyes and in a rather stern tone says, "You listen to me and you listen good. Your mind will do anything you program it to do. If you program it to fail then it will, but on the other hand if you program it to succeed then it will do that also." Such a statement by L.T. transformed Sara from a doubter to believer, she hugs and thanks him.

Then while looking him squarely in the eyes Sara says, "Only the sky could limit your achievements."

L.T. replies, "Thanks, Sis. Now you'd better get ready to touch some sky yourself." Afterwards they smile at one another and go their separate ways.

Reality is the unfolding of destiny one day at a time. Furthermore one would be hard pressed to believe that destiny is what delivers him from the day to day hardships of reality. On this seemly calm day L.T. is surprised by a visitor whose destiny has all but been revealed, in Lazerbeam. As L.T. is about to enter the house for dinner, Lazerbeam approaches him. L.T. immediately notices that Lazerbeam isn't himself, and from Lazerbeam's approach L.T. knows that a change has come over him. Once within ear shot Lazerbeam speaks the greeting of the day. A shocked L.T. returns greetings. Then while staring at the sidewalk Lazerbeam says, "I just want you to know that I think the world of you and I'll be pulling for you to win that contest." A speechless L.T., who doesn't want to be

seen in the company of Lazerbeam for fear it might dis-
qualify him, is unable to move at this particular moment.
Meanwhile Lazerbeam continues his confession saying,
"You know two of my dealers got killed last Friday, and
one was my baby brother." Lazerbeam adds, "I am not asking you to feel sorry for me, but I do want you to know
that that tragedy along with my arrest changed my out
look on life. Daily as I sat in that jail cell I began to reflect
over my life and in the process I was informed by God Almighty that I, much like the biblical character Jonah, had
been running from his calling. Momentarily I realized that
this jail cell is serving as my vehicle for change, much like
that whale did in Jonah's case. Without a doubt I know
that was the cue for me to turn my life over to Christ."

A baffled L.T. had to pinch himself but manages to
maintain his composure. As tears begin to fill the wells of
his eyes Lazerbeam says, "You was a sharp little brother,
now you're a sharp big brother, and someday I know you'll
be a sharp old man." Lazerbeam concludes by saying, "As
for me I just hope to live long enough to get old, because
you see Little Einstein, I'm going to jail. My trial is set to
began around the date they'll announce the winner of the
scholarship contest." Through the avalanche of tears that
now cover his face Lazerbeam looks at L.T. and says, "Just
knowing that you've won that scholarship contest will convince me that for once justice in America will have been
served." Without uttering another sound Lazerbeam turns
and walks away. However, at this time both he and L.T.
are thinking about the same initials, "BMW." These initials when pertaining to black men are most beneficial
when interpreted as Best Methods Win.

It's now the start of the second semester of L.T.'s senior year and up to this point he has been elected student body president and he has also been chosen most
likely to succeed. But more important is the fact that L.T.
still has a 4.0 GPA. A review of his classes and grades
averages reads:

French II	A semester avg.
Physics	A semester avg.
Trigonometry	A semester avg.
Business Computers II	A semester avg.
American Literature	A semester avg.
Economics II (emphasis on micro-economics)	A semester avg.

The second semester marks the point within the contest where the judges release the names of the top three candidates within each division. In division #7, the top candidates are Billy Tubbs, Gail Anderson, and Luther Thompson. Also at this point in the contest, the candidates are to turn in a list of the three colleges they wish to attend. L.T.'s list reads choice #1 Harvard University, choice #2 Harvard University, choice #3 Harvard University. Naturally L.T.'s list prompts the scholarship committee to contact him and question why he made all three choices read the same.

However, before L.T. turned in his list to the committee he and Ms. Johnson also discuss his choices and reasoning. Ms. Johnson, who was caught totally by surprise when L.T. chose all three spots to read the same, challenged him to explain his motive for such actions. Without hesitation he stated, "I only have one choice, I just wrote it three times." He continued saying, "I've reached for the top so long, it's too late now for me to accept anything less." And as soon as L.T. completed his explanation Ms. Johnson leaped to her feet clapping and saying, "Bravo, bravo! I love it!" Furthermore when the committee arrived at L.T.'s school and questioned his choices, again without hesitation L.T. informs them just as he had Ms. Johnson. Now it's not certain if this move won any points with the committee. For L.T., however, the reactions of the committee members indicate that it certainly didn't hurt his chances any.

It's now only five weeks remaining in the contest and the contestants are to physically meet one another and visit each others' homes and schools. Then they are to write a short subjective essay about each of the other contestant's obstacles, if any, and the effects of their surroundings. They are to include their opinion as to how they would have operated had they too been required to function in the others' environment. L.T. is the only contestant from his division who lives in the ghetto. Gail, who's also black, has a father who is a doctor and a mother who is an x-ray technician while Billy is Caucasian and his parents are millionaires. During the visiting phase, it is discovered that inside Billy's room he has an IBM computer with a fax machine too. There is a 6-foot tall bookshelf and on its shelves are books on every topic imaginable. Billy's neighborhood is one that requires security guards at it's entrance, just like Judge Cromwells. Gail's family's neighborhood consists of homes starting at five hundred thousand dollars. Her room is also equipped with a computer and fax capabilities, along with a loaded bookshelf. Gail's school is less than five years old, and each of the past four years a student from her school has won this contest. She like L.T. and Billy carries a 4.0 GPA.

L.T., having visited both Gail's and Billy's homes, neighborhoods, and schools now begins to feel inferior for the first time ever. Needless to say his surroundings, his family's rowhouse, and the condition of his school leaves a lot to be desired. Nonetheless he escorts and informs the two candidates around the areas of interest as proudly as they had shown him around. Afterwards L.T. mentally coaches himself to stand tough and above all else believe in the workload he has amassed.

One week remains in the school year but more importantly, tonight at Radio City Music Hall the scholarship winners will be announced. Today Albert and Thelma, along with thousands of onlookers and parents, family members, and friends across New York, are preparing to attend tonight's ceremony. Muhammad has made the trip in from Chicago and Sara is home on leave from the Air Force as well. Tonight fifteen of the state's division winners will be announced, while next weekend the remaining winners will be identified. L.T., like many other candidates, will have a slew of supporters; the Cromwells, Ms. Johnson, Mrs. Hepburn, Mrs. Parker and many others are filing into the Music Hall where the ceremony will begin in about forty-five minutes. L.T. and his family, along with the old gang of supporters including Vanessa and Charles, are seated together and everyone has already begun to perspire.

The program notes each contestant and their division, chosen college, and major in the order in which they'll be announced. Division Seven candidates reads: Gail Anderson, UCLA, Journalism; Luther Thompson, Harvard, Law; and Billy Tubbs, University of Texas, Political Science. More and more the people flow into the auditorium. Even though thousands are entering there will only be fifteen winners. Judging from the various looks upon many of the faces tonight can produce only one of two outcomes; a dream that has come true or the shattering of dreams. As the time for the ceremony to begin approaches, the auditorium's aura becomes more intense, stress-induced facial features are more pronounced. Anticipation, ringing of the hands, and crossing of the fingers are quickly taking on new meaning.

Gradually the lights are dimmed and suddenly the stage curtain opens, "Good evening ladies and gentlemen, it's showtime," the master of ceremonies announces! Almost on cue thousands of hearts begin fluttering with the probability of heart attack being their proper diagnosis. Upon the completion of the opening prayer and the playing of the national anthem, time has come to announce the winner from Division One. Following the announcement of the first winner, the place erupts with applause, whistles, and screams, but most importantly, tears of joy.

Then the second winner is announced followed by the third, then the fourth also. Division Five winner quoted this phrase through teary eyes during her acceptance speech, "Every worthwhile accomplishment, big or little, has its stages of drudgery and triumph; a beginning, a struggle and a victory!" She then added, "Tonight I have victory. Thank you New York."

Throughout this ceremony L.T. and others witness some obviously needy children both win and lose. Needless to say tears of different sorts are falling like torrential rain on this night. The sixth winner has just been announced but it'll take a few minutes because immediately following the announcement both the winner and her mother fainted. The winner has finally made her way to the stage where she starts her acceptance speech by informing the audience that, "I'm the oldest of my mother's five children." Continuing she adds, "I've never seen my father, but in my mother I still had the equivalent of two parents wrapped up into one. I'm living proof that anyone can achieve anything he or she sets their mind to accomplish, if they only believe in themselves." She closes by saying, "I owe it all to my mother. I love you mother." She then looks skyward to say, "Thank you Lord, thank you New York!" Afterwards the building explodes with applause, whistles, screams, and of course, tears of both joy and sadness.

The time has come for the announcement of Division Seven. The master of ceremony informs the audience, "This was the hardest division of all in which to pick just one winner because all three candidates finished with a 4.0 GPA. The rules committee even sought an exception to the rule. However, the committee's accounting department ruled that it would not be fair to have two winners because the state simply could not afford three scholarships. He then shouts, "Lets give Billy Tubbs, Luther Thompson, and Gail Anderson a great big round of applause!" Such an ovation was given the contestants it seemed as if though the roof would collapse, after a few minutes the PA announcer holds up his hands as a request for silence. In no time at all the Music Hall becomes quiet enough to hear a cotton ball hit the floor. The speaker then announces, "And the winner from Division Seven is Luther Thompson!"

Thelma and Ms. Johnson's screams couldn't have been better-timed had they planned them! Both seemed to scream at the same time so loud they nearly shattered the auditorium windows! Albert begins shaking uncontrollably, Judge and Mrs. Cromwell both become flushed with emotion. Meanwhile L.T. calmly makes his way to the stage. He begins his acceptance speech saying, "Thank you Mama and Daddy. Thank you Ms. Johnson, Judge and Mrs. Cromwell along with so many more who's names are too many to mention." L.T. then adds, "For years various people dear to me have taught me the true meaning of two very important phrases. One is by Confucius which reads, 'Our greatest glory is not in never falling, but in rising every time we fall.' And the other is an old Chinese proverb which reads, 'Give a man a fish, and you feed him for a day. Teach a man to fish, and you feed him for a lifetime.'" L.T. closes by looking skyward and saying, "Thank you Lord, and Thank you New York!" Afterwards applause again roars throughout the building.

Once back at his seat, L.T. is swamped with hugs and kisses from all of the gang. The ceremony continues right along until its completion. Afterwards Gail congratulates L.T. and wishes him the best and L.T. wishes her likewise. However Billy wants L.T. to know one thing which he says, "If you were not a poor black ghetto boy you wouldn't have won, but instead I would have won." Billy vows to have his parents look into the quality of classes L.T. has taken, starting from the ninth grade onward. Having spoken his peace Billy leaves without another word. However, L.T. departs as division winner and with his sights set on attending Harvard.

7 *SENSE OF UNREST*

Throughout one's life we must first envision our destiny. It has been said that the future doesn't start tomorrow it begins today. Visions can hold us! Visions make up fifty percent of a person's goals. America has numerous citizens whose vision and ideology must be implemented into its society if America is to experience its full potential and continue to be recognized across the globe as the world's leader. James Weldon Johnson once said, "Every race and every nation should be judged by the best it has been able to produce, not by the worst." Perhaps one day in this nation such ideology will have high priority.

The sunshine penetrating the faded blue curtains produces a serene setting throughout the room resulting in an atmosphere conducive for recollection. This morning as L.T. awakens, the first object his eyes focus upon is his scholarship certificate propped against the mirror on the dresser. Wham! At that moment L.T. develops an urge to mentally massage his collective conscience as ugly images attempt to bombard his mind. A peek into the window of L.T.'s mind reveals his desire to examine numerous cultural annotations instrumental in producing changes.

He begins by analyzing an old cliché that pertains to the definition of insanity. It reads something like this: "A man is insane if he keeps doing the same thing over and over again and expects different results." Such phrases confirm L.T.'s belief that mere exposure to particular circumstances during the course of one's life can produce equally valuable benefits for overcoming life's dilemmas in much the same manner that physical encounters can. Momentarily he gives some thought to the four places (the church, gymnasium, bank, and library) that Thelma asked he forever utilize for their benefits. Then in a methodical fashion L.T. repeats the two myths Albert spoke of saying, "Blacks can only obtain fame and notoriety through either music, comedy or sports but not through academics. Blacks don't dedicate themselves to the point where they're driven to success."

Afterwards L.T. begins to recollect many of his life's trials. In doing so, he thinks of this phrase, "Life's battles don't always go to the stronger or faster man; but sooner or later the man who wins is the man who thinks he can." On the other hand L.T. hopes that he doesn't become someone who learns the importance of an intended lesson of life after reality has amplified the issue and/or topic in question. He knows full well that most blacks are beset by shifting ideologies and superficial conclusions. Even though L.T. has only graduated from high school, he despises terms such as "vicious cycle of poverty" and "dependency syndrome," because they are nothing more than political factors which prevents blacks at the bottom from moving upward. Furthermore, having disproved the theory of his mental inferiority, from this moment onward L.T. seriously intends to use all of his time wisely.

There is a bittersweet element that governs all of our lives, which serves as preserver of the past, cradle of the present, and caretaker of the future; that element happens to be father time. Time to the affluent in America and throughout the world sings a tune of sweet harmony. However, to procrastinators, the less fortunate, minorities of color he echoes a bitter phrase, "Dreams can't compare to goals already achieved." L.T. knows full well that solutions to his plight and those of minorities in general will not be easily identified, but this doesn't signify that they are impossible to achieve. Recognizing the numerous complexities as challenges rather than obstacles will allow all who challenge such huge tasks to make progress, if they freely admit they have no magic.

L.T. is fully aware that today signifies the start of a new beginning in that he is now entering another phase of this thing called life. It is with the understanding of the old saying, "Life doesn't owe you anything simply because you're here." Then L.T. moves forward in accordance with the term living. L.T.'s attitude and self-confidence won't be affected by insensitive interpreters of the constitution but will be fueled by his attempts to emulate his role models. Moreover, since criminal records may foreclose future options the topic is certain to be one of great interest as he attempts to climb the ladder of life rung by rung. Even though L.T. wants to succeed more than anything else in this world, he knows full well the meaning of this old Chinese proverb, "The gem cannot be polished without friction, nor man perfected without trials."

Since graduation is completed the task that now lies ahead is college, but first L.T.'s off to work at the Cromwells as usual. Upon his arrival L.T. is ushered onto the patio by Vanessa. There he is officially presented with the promised eight thousand dollar trust fund, and a Visa credit card as well. Needless to say the term grateful doesn't come close to defining L.T.'s feelings at this particular moment. Nonetheless he hugs and thanks both the Judge and Carolyn what seem to have been a hundred times before going off and attending to his work.

Completion of today's work can't be accomplished fast enough because L.T. can't wait to tell his parents about his extraordinary gift. Upon L.T.'s arrival home a stunned Thelma has to grab a hold of her heart shortly after he bursts through the door shouting, "Mama, Mama!" Once everyone's attention is focused on him L.T. shows them his credit card and trust fund certificate. Thelma shows her approval by jumping up and down while nearly squeezing the life out of L.T. Meanwhile Albert tries to congratulate him by merely shaking his hand but quickly drops the macho image and pulls L.T. into a bearhug. They all soon regain their composure and discuss in depth the meaning of this significant gift. The discussion ends with everyone in agreement that L.T. attending college is a suitable reward for his dedication to school.

Having disclosed and discussed the Cromwells graduation gift with his parents, L.T. runs off to visit Ms. Johnson. A joyful Ms. Johnson meets L.T. at the door and soon after he's seated she presents him with another graduation gift in the form of a new IBM PS2 computer and printer. Again this gift sends L.T. on an emotional rollercoaster as he hugs and thanks Ms. Johnson nearly to death. She assures him of two things; one being he deserves it, another being, that at Harvard he'll need it also. After sufficient celebration by L.T., the two of them discuss some future plans before Ms. Johnson drives an ecstatic L.T. home. Immediately upon their entrance to the house carrying boxes containing the computer parts, celebration starts once again. After L.T. brings in the printer, everyone gathers at the kitchen table for a brief discussion before Ms. Johnson departs. This summer Lady Luck is smiling down on the Thompsons like never before. On this day a jubilant Albert has just burst into the house to tell Thelma, "I have been named district representative!" Once Albert gets a hold of himself he informs Thelma, "Now I can move you out of this ghetto and into a small house in the suburbs."

Naturally learning of this news moves Thelma to tears. The following days tension grows as the task of house hunting grows difficult. For a while Thelma thinks perhaps the task might not be accomplished. But after relentless searching and some prudent negotiating, the Thompsons find a new affordable home. The new surroundings will take some getting use too but no one is complaining.

Daily the simmering hot summer heat nearly softens the paved streets, meanwhile L.T. is in his room practicing on his computer, attempting to master every function key available. In approximately one week L.T. has to report to Harvard. On this Saturday ,L.T. has decided it's time to officially begin his farewell visits with close friends as well as a few trips to some fond places. First it's off to the Schomburg Center for a visit with Mrs. Hepburn. Once there he immediately makes eye contact with her. Afterwards the two of them move over to a quiet area and begin to reminisce. Nearly an hour later the two embrace and wish one another good luck before L.T. departs.

On this particular Monday morning the sunlight cuts through an uncharacteristically cool breeze as L.T. exits the metro en route to the Cromwells. He joins the Cromwells for breakfast during which L.T. is given some sound advice as well as is informed of the enormous expectations of him which he feels he is capable of fulfilling. After breakfast he's off to spend some time with Ms. Johnson and right away she begins a thought-stimulating conversation with him in preparation for L.T.'s departure to Harvard. She begins by asking, "What's the first building you're going to locate once you get settled into your dorm?"

A perplexed L.T. in a guessing manner answers, "The library."

Ms. Johnson in a stern tone replies, "You're darn right." She then asks, "What's your purpose for attending Harvard?"

Again an uncertain L.T. replies, "To dispel numerous demoralizing myths that pertain to this African-American offspring."

After that answer Ms. Johnson nods her head in agreement and then changes the subject to a more relaxing topic, much to L.T.'s delight! The two then chat for about an hour before L.T.'s departure.

Today while passing his old middle school L.T. has to chuckle to himself as he stops and stands peeking through the holes of the fence that enclose the track and football field. Momentarily L.T. remembers the conversation between him and Coach Washington pertaining to his inability to play a team sport. After a reasonable amount of time, L.T. moves on to visit a few other fond places like Central Park and the bookstand before going home.

Today is bittersweet for L.T. because it's the day prior to his leaving for Boston. First of all, he's off to the Cromwells where upon his arrival L.T. notices everyone's misty eyes. Nonetheless well wishes and conversation fill the patio and its surroundings until L.T. announces his departure. Afterwards Carolyn's and Vanessa's tears become visible while the Judge and Charles manage to hold theirs back. In spite of it all, L.T. hugs everyone and they exchange their goodbyes and wishes of good luck. A visibly saddened Vanessa walks L.T. to the door.

L.T.'s heart begins to pound more pronounced than ever before. He even begins to feel weak as he approaches Ms. Johnson's door. Nonetheless he manages to ring the door bell and from the moment she opens the front door a mixture of happiness and sadness blankets Ms. Johnson's face.

Once in the sitting room their conversation is filled with memories of old times. They also reiterate their understanding regarding L.T.'s present and future goals. Ms. Johnson draws strength to carry on as the closest individual to the son she never had walks to the door. There the two of them bear hug one another and even shed tears before L.T.'s departure.

The time has come for L.T. to leave for Boston. Albert and Thelma will accompany him to the airport. They invite Ms. Johnson but she said she could not stand to see L.T. leave therefore she declined. Charles has the Judge's permission to chauffeur L.T. and his parents to the airport. Once at the airport the scene is a sad yet joyous occasion for the Thompsons. Needless to say before L.T. boards the aircraft everyone including Charles agrees that at this time in L.T.'s life attending college is the best move. In spite of it all, Thelma cannot hold back her tears as her baby walks to board that airplane. Meanwhile light tears of joy roll down Albert's cheeks also.

The flight serves as a new and exhilarating experience for L.T. once he gets over the take-off jitters and the plane levels off. However, the occasional turbulence generates a new form of uncertainty. But through it all including the bumpy landing L.T. has become a much better person for having accepted the challenge to fly versus catching the bus. Upon his arrival to Harvard, L.T. is strictly business with a bit of apprehension to boot until he gets assigned and settled inside his dorm room.

L.T. will be rooming with Henry Reed, a white kid from Michigan. Henry stands approximately six feet tall, weighs around 200 pounds, has red curly hair and a face full of freckles. Henry and L.T. introduce themselves and spend some time getting to know one another. During their get-acquainted session Henry confides in L.T., "I'm scared to death of the University's demands to include the professors because my sister flunked out midway her junior year." Henry continues saying, "According to Mary, studying is a sixteen hour a day requirement, because she was studying fourteen hours in order to pass the demanding courses while trying to sleep eight hours, and using the remaining two for daily routine, but that philosophy didn't work."

L.T. notices that Henry is making himself upset so he suggests, "Why don't we take a walk around campus?" to which Henry agrees. Henry knew where a lot of the buildings were on campus because he and his parents had visited Mary occasionally. Henry even knew of a few places off campus to go and not to visit which he informed L.T. about of course. Now as they stroll around campus chatting and becoming better acquainted L.T. learns that Henry's major is political science. Henry also confides in L.T., "Someday I hope to become the Governor of Michigan."

L.T. has discovered by this time that Henry needs a little assurance. Therefore, L.T. assures Henry, "All you have to do is to believe in yourself and the governorship is already won." Henry liked that way of thinking and thanked L.T. for that vote of confidence. Afterwards they return to the dorm and phone their families to assure them that all is well so far.

The daylight has given away to the darkness meanwhile, L.T. and Henry prepare for bed. Shortly after Henry, who's bed is closest to the door, turns off the light switch. He's under the covers and sound asleep. On the other hand L.T. can only toss and turn. Nearly an hour later L.T.'s still unable to get to sleep so he decides to go out for a walk in the night air. He throws off the sheet and rolls over to the side of bed and sits up for a moment. L.T. then gets out of bed and goes into the bathroom and simultaneously closes the door behind himself. L.T. then turns on the light and stares into the mirror where he sees the reflection of an ambitious black teenager. He momentarily turns on the sink's cold water, splashes a little onto his face, and quickly towel dries his face. Once again L.T. looks into the mirror before easing over to his clothes that are draped across the chair at his work desk which he grabs and puts on and then slips on his shoes. In his effort not to awake Henry, L.T. quietly walks over to the door and eases it open. As he steps out into the hallway the door closes.

Now outside and strolling along the halls of this historical university, L.T.'s mind begin to run at a pace of a mile a minute. He thinks of how wonderful it will be to be known as an African-American who graduated from Harvard. L.T. feels that to be associated with previous graduates from this institution simply can't be explained. As he continues strolling about campus, L.T.'s pride swells to overflowing as he visualizes how the sound of someone describing him as a ghetto-born black who challenged Harvard and won (graduated) will sound like music to his ears. Having gotten somewhat carried away with his fantasizing L.T. suddenly realizes that he is about four blocks off campus. This he knows because over there is a place which earlier today Henry warned him to stay away from. Nevertheless he decides to at least familiarize himself with some of the surrounding areas off campus, but not that place.

Therefore, L.T. decides to head back towards campus so he turns down a dim lit street in an attempt to at least learn the area he has travelled tonight. Then suddenly seemly from out of nowhere two black guys sprint past L.T. Once they pass him the two split up and run down the alley ways. No sooner do the guys pass L.T. when he hears the sound of sirens approaching. Before L.T. can travel five yards a policeman yells, "Halt!" Unaware that the officer is talking to him, L.T. keeps walking until he hears the officer say, "Halt you son-of-a-bitch or I'll blast your ass if that left foot of yours even touches the ground." A terrified L.T. quickly freezes in his tracks with his left leg bent in mid air. One of the two policemen then command, "Assume the position!"

A trembling L.T. questions, "What have I done officer?" L.T. then lowers his left leg and right away he hears the sound of the policemen's guns cock. Needless to say L.T. saw his life flash before his very eyes.

From that moment on it seems as if though this whole ordeal is a dream and any minute now his mother will awake him. But the tone of the policeman's voice is all too real as he tells his partner, "Cover me while I search him." With their revolvers still drawn and pointed squarely at the back of L.T.'s skull, the officer in charge then orders him, "Turn around and spread eagle against that wall." Afterwards the lead officer places his weapon in his holster as he walks up and searches L.T. As he frisks L.T., the policeman questions him asking, "You niggers are all alike, what you thought that by splitting up that we wouldn't catch you is that it?" The officer's thick Boston accent seems to add to the authority he already holds. Meanwhile a bewildered L.T. is speechless.

At this time trembling is the major force that allowed L.T. to move at all, and once he felt those cold handcuffs tighten around his wrists even that movement became harder to produce. As L.T. and the policemen walk towards the squad car the officer in charge sarcastically reads him his rights. Once in the backseat of the patrol car and learning of the charges (breaking and entering, attempted rape, communicating a threat and assault with a deadly weapon) L.T.'s brain waves start to search for a possible solution to his dilemma. Having examined the situation his mind advises him to do just one thing— pray. Without hesitation L.T. sends up a request to God.

Upon arrival to the station his fears are rekindled even though L.T. has been praying. As he is ushered into the station and the booking procedures begin, hopelessness fills his entire soul. And judging from L.T.'s observation of the station's occupants, everyone assumes that since he got arrested he has committed the crime. Before tonight L.T. had not really known to what depths his father was trying to get him to understand that his present situation is one that numerous blacks experience daily, even though they too are no more a criminal than he is tonight. Moving right along with the booking procedures, L.T.'s hands and fingers are being prepared for fingerprinting. Upon completion he's ordered over to the camera and given a name board and various pictures are taken. Afterwards he is allowed to make his phone call.

Suddenly terror becomes the number one force controlling L.T.'s bodily functions as he realizes that he has no one he can call at this time. A disturbed L.T. informs the policeman of his predicament. Without remorse the jailing officer leads L.T. away to a cell. The jailer walks past two cells that contain only one white man in each to later stop and open one with five black occupants. The sight of the cell occupants immediately triggers L.T.'s mind to recall a statement Judge Cromwell once told him: a man is not defeated by his opponents but by himself.

Shortly after the officer locks the cell door, L.T.'s mind begins to visualize and pray about the proceeding that is to take place in about six hours. Cautiously L.T.'s eyes scan the cell and notice that all of the others are asleep which makes him feel a little at ease. But nothing could or would ease his mind like getting out of here because mandatory briefings and seminars that freshmen must attend start tomorrow. L.T. slowly sinks into an unexplainable state of depression as the sound of the clock down the hall seems to tick his life away. Then as he mulls over his predicament he tries to convince himself that there is no way he will be picked out of that line up tomorrow. Moreover he wishes that it wasn't so early (2 a.m.) so that he could do this line up thing right this minute.

As time ticks on more and more L.T. acts out scenes of himself serving as his own lawyer. With his biggest defense being the line up, he is certain that once the victimized family saw him they would clear him, especially since he is not the criminal. "That's it," L.T. thinks to himself,

"Within my dilemma is my solution." He feels that since the family has never seen him, there's no way they will say he's the perpetrator. Throughout the remainder of the early morning L.T. tries to psyche himself into believing that he will be released in a matter of time. Therefore he sums up his situation in this manner saying, "Bad timing got me into this mess, but in time it will be time that gets me out of this mess too." As time passes the inmates begin awaking and before long they and L.T. exchange arrest stories. Needless to say they do not believe L.T. when he tells them he is a freshman at Harvard with his major being law. Nonetheless they all have one thing in common—occupying this jail cell.

It's now eight a.m. The time has come for L.T. and the others to be moved out and positioned into the line up. As they are ushered into position, L.T. prays a silent prayer because he knows that this is his only way out of this mess. Once they are into position, the officer in charge orders them to, "Turn to the left." Then he calls L.T.'s position saying, "Prisoner number three, step forward, turn to the right side, step back." After approximately fifteen minutes all the others are ushered back to the cell while L.T. is left alone. He is then informed by the officer that he needs to get prepared to meet with his lawyer because he has been identified as the criminal who committed the crimes of which he's accused. A bewildered L.T. nearly fainting in disbelief is the best description for him at this moment.

Suddenly L.T. hears a little girl crying while inquiring to her mother, "Mommy how could you say he's the one when you know that wasn't one of the men who attacked us?" The girl, who's twelve years old is putting her parents teachings of right and wrong to the test. Darlene even describes the two attackers in detail and neither description comes close to L.T.'s features. Needless to say a perplexed L.T. wonders is anyone listening to this little girl? Apparently not because he is still being ushered on down the hallway and into a briefing room to be introduced to his court-appointed lawyer. Now overcome by grief L.T. appears helpless as his lawyer enters the room, so much so that the lawyer backs out of the room without saying a word and closes the door. He personally knows that L.T.'s display of grief is not the profile of as hardened a criminal as the charges indicate.

Meanwhile little Darlene Morganheimer is still questioning her parents, "Mother why falsely accuse that man, when you know he wasn't one of the attackers?" The lawyer overhears Darlene's request and therefore he approaches the family to question them. Soon after he introduces himself and informs the family of L.T.'s display of grief. He assures them that the man they have identified isn't a strong armed criminal. "See, see I told you so mommy. That wasn't one of the men that attacked us," Darlene shouts.

Dan quickly orders his daughter to, "Hush up right now!" He then adds, "That nigger has got to pay for what happened to your mother!"

Darlene states, "But Daddy they didn't rape us but they did scare the heck out of us. I could see if mom and I had been raped or injured or something but we weren't."

Darlene continues saying, "You and mom have always taught me and Tommy to tell the truth and now you two are lying, even though you know an innocent man can go to jail, and I just can't understand why."

Dan again orders his daughter, "Hush up now or you're grounded for life!" He adds, "That nigger is going to pay the price for the ones that got away."

Having heard enough, the lawyer pleads for the Morganheimer family to shatter the myths that all blacks are evil. Mrs. Morganheimer then speaks up saying, "You're right. We shouldn't make him pay if he really isn't the guilty party. I'm not going to press charges. Tell your client we're sorry."

She then looks down at a proud Darlene who says, "Mommy I knew you couldn't falsely accuse an innocent man." Darlene then positions herself between her parents and grabs a hold of each one's hand then leads them out the door. Afterwards the lawyer returns to the briefing room and informs a distraught L.T. that the family changed their minds and they aren't going to file any charges. A jubilant L.T. jumps up from the table and thanks the lawyer nearly a thousand times. At which time the lawyer informs L.T. ,"You've just benefitted from the shattering of a myth." He then orders L.T., "Follow me as I go out to the desk and clear up this matter properly." Of course a relieved L.T. is more than happy to comply.

Upon arrival to campus while getting out of the car, a relieved L.T. thanks his lawyer for the ride and for the advice also. L.T. quickly runs up to his dorm room where he showers and changes clothes. The time is approximately noon and L.T. hopes Henry will return to the room so that he can brief him about the morning's events and inform him of what's up for the afternoon. Sure enough a worried Henry returns to the room in search of L.T. Once Henry comes through the door, the two of them are relieved to see one another again. Henry immediately asks, "Where have you been? I've been worried sick about you?"

L.T. replies, "I got lost last night during my walk in an attempt to feel the night air because I couldn't get to sleep."

Henry replies, "Well it's no time to sleep now. We've got just enough time to grab some lunch and get to our next scheduled briefing."

A relieved L.T. grabs his bookbag and beats Henry out of the door.

It has been a long week of both seminars and briefings, but a grateful L.T. is simply glad to have been free to attend them. L.T. has decided to stay on campus this weekend which is the last one before classes starts on Monday. He still hasn't told anyone about his trying experience due in part to his belief that by not discussing it, it will be forgotten quicker. Ring-a-ding! On this Monday morning the sound of the alarm clock is like music to L.T.'s ears considering where he was last Monday morning. Without hesitation he and Henry get up and prep for their first day of college.

Wow! A stunned L.T. is shocked at the size of the class— not the classroom but the number of students. There must be over three hundred students in here. Slowly he and Henry walk down the aisle to some empty seats about midway and take their seats. Once the bell rings and L.T. and Henry begin changing classes, L.T. again experiences another facet of college life —changing classes can be murder. The bell signaling the end of the day has a rather melodious ring to it from L.T.'s point of view. Once back at the dorm, both Henry and L.T. sprawl out across their beds but only for a minute, because both are in disbelief that after the first day they have homework from every class.

Nearly two weeks have passed and tonight L.T. and Henry are in a discussion with some of the older students who are sharing some of the school's fairy tales about various professors. The student doing most of the talking is a junior who has had two years of classes from the professors the students refer to as the big three. They are professors Spelman, Thorpe, and Webster. Professor Spelman is the most feared and respected professor on campus because the unspoken rule is if Professor Spelman's classes don't get you then you'll graduate. Most of the students have their stories to tell about their years under Spelman. Professor Spelman is a tall man with a medium build and pure white hair. He has an overall distinguished look about him that just makes anyone who comes in contact with him respect him.

A student's major determines how many years someone has to study under various professors. Political science, Henry's major, requires only two years under those professors. On the other hand, L.T. is a little disturbed by the fact that his entire four years will have to be spent under the big three. Professor Webster is known to ask for or even give a test on material up to three chapters ahead of what's being studied by the class at the present time. Professor Webster is a tall bald-headed heavy built man who speaks with a deep voice. He's known for his reputation of failing the kids of celebrities. It was once rumored around campus that professor Webster sent the president of Yale University's son home with a note that read, "Only at Yale would this paper be acceptable. Unfortunately for you your son attends Harvard and at Harvard this paper warrants the letter grade 'F'." It later became known to be just a rumor but the reputation stands. As for Professor Thorpe, the word on him is that he teaches psychology in and out of the classroom. Professor Thorpe's classes require never-ending quests for answers to questions and different psychological methods for improving America's everyday lifestyles. Some of the students say the professor is so smart he borders on the brink of genius and idiot. Naturally hearing these stories manages to knock some of the wind from L.T.'s sails but he still feels that if students before him managed to pass these men's classes then so will he.

Today on this Friday afternoon L.T.'s phone call to Ms. Johnson provides him with just the boost he needs in order to continue to think positively. Throughout the year L.T. shares Thelma's concept of visiting the four places with Henry, and each time L.T. visits a facility Henry tags along. It isn't certain if their visits to the library, gym, bank, and church result in both L.T. and Henry carrying grade point averages of 3.48 at the end of the first semester, but, if asked neither would say that the visits hurt them.

8 *PLANTING SEEDS*

Racial intolerance is one of the greatest shames of mankind on this planet earth. However, for many minorities of color, day-to-day existence in America has a way of manipulating their mental capabilities in such a manner that the term logic simply kindles the existing chaos. Such hardships are due in part to the offsprings of this nation's forefathers interpretation of a document (the Constitution), that perhaps is too elaborate for this nation's governing bodies to properly translate. Therefore, the multiple forms of discrimination in various cases are festered by the teachings of perpetrators whose motives are different, yet the term culprit unites them all.

Never in L.T.'s wildest imagination could he have imagined how chores like laundry and keeping one's room clean could become such a time-consuming necessity. That is until he tried getting around not doing any of them because he and Henry seem to forever have a need to stop studying and do daily chores. Nonetheless L.T. loves the challenges that comes with attending college and as the year progresses, he and Henry have grown to rely on one another. Besides by doing so they've begun to believe in the possibility that they might complete this first year after all. Some nine months later and having withstood the numerous cram sessions and the frightening pop quizzes as well as the endless nights of studying until the break of dawn, L.T. has finally completed his first year at Harvard.

Now that classes have ended for the year it will still be another six weeks before L.T. goes home because he has accepted the challenge to travel and study abroad. L.T. believes that a person should get a complete education which he thinks includes knowledge about foreign affairs. Therefore he has signed up to join the University's program that allows a certain number of students to participate in cultural studies. Beginning the first six weeks of the summer, the students are tutored as they visit three countries. While visiting the students will study the social, political and economic conditions within each country. They will spend approximately ten days in each country. This year they will visit China, France, and West Germany.

Today the first item of business on L.T.'s agenda is for him to see off his classmates who are on their way home. After the last goodbye, L.T. phones Thelma, Ms. Johnson, and the Cromwells one last time before his flight out in the morning. Afterwards L.T. returns to his room where he excitedly makes sure to pack his tape recorder, camera, and plenty of film along with enough writing materials which he hopes will last the entire trip. L.T. then places his bags near the door and beds down for the night.

The following morning he is up and dressed quickly because the group is to be at the airport no later than eight a.m.; needless to say L.T. arrives in plenty of time. It should be mentioned that after all of the check-in procedures are completed, this time as L.T. boards the airplane he is looking forward to the flight.

Finally the long flight is over and upon arrival in China, L.T. who had never been out of New York state prior to attending college, is all eyes and ears as the students and chaperones exit the plane. Because L.T. is the only black student in the group, curiosity surrounds him from the moment he exits the plane. The students are led to a tour bus and they are then driven from the airport by way of the scenic route to their hotel. Naturally all of the students are snapping away with their cameras as the bus rolls through the streets. Some two hours later the students are informed of their agenda, which includes three visits to China's White House where they will be involved in political discussions. Night has crept up on the city and the students, who are in groups of eight, are observing the events along the streets. L.T. sees the activities as a far cry from those on the streets of Harlem. Around ten p.m. the students return to their room as they are eager to witness history in the makings.

This morning as the sun is rising over Peking provides all who witness it a breathtaking sight. The audience includes a energized L.T. who is awake attempting to capture the sunrise with both his mind's eye and that of his camera. After breakfast and a briefing the students are driven to China's White House to learn how the country's government works on a daily basis. During the time of the students' arrival the topic being debated is the judicial system and young new wave politicians are having their voices for change heard on the floor at this time. But it doesn't look like the young party will be able to obtain enough votes to change the present structure. L.T. is very attentive as he observes the facial expressions upon the faces of the elder Chinese spokesmen as the young representative vehemently explains his party's points of view. There is no doubt that witnessing these events will enlighten all of the students in attendance.

It is now five days into the tour and this morning the House members will allow the American students to join in discussion, at which time the students will have the freedom to speak freely, as well as answer questions presented to them. The session opens with the students being informed of how daily business is conducted in the House. Afterwards the floor is open for discussion, at which time a few students inquire about the political practices within China which lasts until lunch. The afternoon session allows time for questions to be asked of the students by members of China's Government. At this time, numerous questions are directed to L.T. as many of the Chinese politician's seem curious as to the plight of blacks in America and the topic of women rights. Therefore, the majority of the House members seek the opinions of the students regarding the conflicting signals America's politicians convey regarding its policies within these areas. The majority of the questions are directed to L.T. and the few female students. The responses given by L.T. make him a sought after man for poses after the formal discussion end and members of the House pose with the students for pictures. Both the nature and number of questions asked of L.T. serve as an enlightening experience he will never forget. The required participation of L.T. will certainly prove beneficial in his quest for knowledge of overseas affairs and opinions that involve the United States. The allotted time to be spent in China has come to an end and the students are boarding the airplane for France.

Upon arrival in Paris the students are escorted to the chartered bus and driven to the hotel via the scenic route. Again everyone is snapping away with their cameras during their attempts to gather lasting memories. Once settled into their rooms, the students are briefed and then allowed to tour Paris. The night life in France is totally different from that of Peking. The students' cameras are as busy as their mouths while they roam the tourist sites and some of the fluent French speaking students enjoy talking with the native citizens. This time during the discussion phase of the tour L.T. isn't bombarded with questions. However, he was asked enough questions to be mentioned. This visit to Paris has allowed L.T. to view first hand how other parts of the world perceive the American-born black man. Needless to say this and other experiences along the way have served to make the trip well worth the taking. The time in Paris seems to fly as it is now time for the students to depart for West Germany.

Frankfurt sort of won over L.T. from the moment he stepped foot into the airport as the native citizens seem so friendly. The tour guide quickly led the students to their bus which impressed L.T. because it was manufactured by Mercedes-Benz. As the bus rolls through the streets the picture-taking routine continues as L.T. and the other students can't get over how clean the streets are. Upon arrival to the hotel the students are met by German students who will assist them as they travel about the city. The dinner meal consists of all German dishes and L.T. loves every bite. As the students and their tutors dine, everyone discusses any and everything that comes to mind. But afterwards L.T. and a number of the other students have to go directly to bed because the silent yet drunken affects of the German beer have gotten the best of them.

The following morning L.T. and the others feel better now that they have slept off the beer and its effects. After breakfast it is right to the streets as the students stroll about taking in the sites and trying out their ability to communicate with the German citizens. The discovery of anything new simply makes the students' interests even broader. L.T. couldn't have imagined how incomplete his education would have been had he not taken this tour. To have learned some of Europe's common customs has allowed L.T. to capture many educational shortcomings that no longer escape him. Such a personal triumph is evident as L.T. diligently jots down notes, records sessions, and snaps pictures of historical landmarks.

The study of Germany's political system teaches the students just how important it is for various countries to consider the condition of their allies. This point is mentioned because of the fall of the Berlin wall and how the effects reuniting the country have resulted in the overall living conditions. The various sessions that the students spend witnessing the German government at work are enlightening even though the format is informal so that the students might have more chance for input. With Frankfurt being the last stop on the tour, L.T. and some of the others take a little time out to visit a few of the night clubs as they learn of the German's social lifestyle. It is time to return to the States and all the students agree that their two thousand dollars was well spent.

As the plane cuts through the blue skies, L.T. takes a moment to reflect upon what this trip meant to him. First of all he is thankful of the Cromwells for the trust fund because without it he would not have been able to afford the trip. This line of thinking is what brings L.T. to ponder the fact that financial planning is a must because without it, limitless opportunities will certainly be lost. L.T. reflects back to the aura of the three countries he and the others have visited and while doing so he can't help but wonder why the U.S.A. doesn't have that aura of "justice at all cost"? Nonetheless L.T. concludes that the trip has filled a big void within his life in that it provided him with a firsthand account of how three of America's allies address and solve critical issues.

Upon his arrival back into the States, L.T. doesn't leave the airport but immediately boards a plane for New York. He is welcomed home with a great big kiss from Thelma and a bearhug from Albert. During the drive to the house L.T. begins to tell his parents about his tour which he has to continue later because the distance from the airport doesn't provide him with enough time. L.T. greets Pam and Toby while unpacking and putting away his things. It isn't long before L.T. telephones Ms. Johnson and the Cromwells. Afterwards he visits them and while at the Cromwells he learns that the Judge has gotten him a summer job not at the house but at a local bank. It doesn't take L.T. long before he gets out of the visiting mode and into the work mode.

L.T.'s job is ideal because it allows him all the time he needs in order to both work and relax. The job also proves beneficial in that it paves the way for him to meet some of the local bankers and learn of banking procedures. The summertime has to be the fastest moving time of the year especially if you are a student, be it high school or college. Nonetheless this summer has served to open L.T.'s eyes and expand his mind to a number of goings-on throughout the world. But just as sure as summer begins, it ends too. The trips to the airport are getting a little easier for Thelma but she still cries whenever L.T.'s plane takes off.

The time has come once again for L.T. and his fellow college mates to get back into the grindstone of college life. This year L.T.'s roommate is Frank Taylor from Springfield, Illinois. Frank is a freshman who's as apprehensive as he can be. Frank is a lanky 6'6" guy with blond hair and blue eyes, with a complexions as pale as snow. Shortly after L.T. and Frank meet and agree upon the room arrangements, L.T. then escorts Frank down to Henry's room where he introduces the two along with Steve who's Henry's roommate. Henry quickly takes this opportunity to inform Frank, "You will be alright if you listen to L.T. and follow his lead."

A modest L.T. says to Frank, "I'll only butt in if you ask. If not then I'll stay out of your business." Frank assures L.T. that he'll be happy for any advice and if L.T. doesn't volunteer enough then Frank will ask him to.

During this little get-acquainted session it is discovered that Frank's major is political science and that he, much like Henry, someday hopes to become governor of his home state. Later L.T. informs Frank about some general information regarding life in the dorm, classes and of course, the big three professors. With the passing of time, Frank and L.T.'s friendship grows as does Henry and Steve's. The four occasionally study together for tests in the classes of the big three and when time permits, they cruise around town in Steve's convertible Mustang. L.T. is really giving it all he's got in the classes of the big three, but with so many students it seems as if he's just one in the number.

It's now the beginning of the second semester which L.T. begins with a 3.40 grade point average. However, the winter months seem to keep him with a cold but illness doesn't keep him out of class. In the usual uninteresting fashion the months pass, inevitably leading into the holiday season. This holiday season is a welcome break for L.T. who misses Thelma's sweet potato pies and other holiday dishes. The northeast is known for its snowy winters and this year is no exception but the snow does let up enough for L.T.'s plane to land. It is without saying that as L.T. enters the terminal as usual Thelma's face lights up like a Christmas tree and as she gets close enough to her baby she nearly squeezes the life out of him.

Upon his arrival home and as soon as L.T. has unpacked he goes directly into the kitchen where he helps himself to the prepared dishes. Afterwards he phones Ms. Johnson and the Cromwells and exchanges small talk. L.T. then unloads the dirty laundry for Thelma to wash as most college students do upon their arrival home. L.T. then settles into a routine of assisting Pam and Toby with their homework while occasionally talking with his parents. Needless to say he also visits both Ms. Johnson and the

Cromwells. The holiday shopping is hectic as usual but along with Pam and Toby, the three of them manage to get it done. Christmas Day everyone exchanges gifts and celebrates; they even talk on the telephone with Sara and Muhammad and all is well. The day after New Years, L.T. returns to college.

A few of the students miss a couple of days due to the weather but everyone eventually makes it back safely. Once back into the routine, Frank and L.T. burn the midnight oil studying. Meanwhile during the day they're swallowing their lunches almost without chewing or tasting the food. L.T. and some of the other minority students on campus meet once weekly just to discuss issues and get to know one another. Some of the upper class minorities notice L.T.'s leadership qualities and from time to time they all encourage each other to go all out in pursuit of their goals. One event after another comes and goes spring break, Easter Holiday and through it all as the school year rolls along so too does the workload. Although, all of these events must come to pass before the semester can end, eventually they come and go resulting in the school year drawing to a close. With the year coming to an end, an excited L.T. has again signed up for the summer tour abroad. L.T. even manages to talk both Henry and Frank into taking the trip.

This year the students group will visit Japan, Korea, and Moscow, and again L.T. prepares by packing his trusty tape recorder, camera and film and of course note pads and pens. Before boarding the airplane, L.T. discovers that unlike last year he isn't the only black student on this trip. There is a female student named Olivia Robinson who'll be traveling along. As for L.T. it is love at first sight. Olivia, who is also entering her junior year this coming fall, has decided to take this opportunity to travel abroad sensing the need to be aware of foreign policy. From takeoff L.T. is trying to get seated next to Olivia which he manages once the young lady sitting beside Olivia falls for L.T.'s line—

that Henry, the guy whom he is seating next to, is begging for the two of them to exchange seats.

Following their introduction L.T. and Olivia strike up a conversation that begins in the usual manner with one another telling select things about themselves to include the trying school years. Olivia has honey brown-colored skin and she stands about 5'5" tall with a well-toned body due to running track during high school and continuing to exercise. She weighs approximately 120 pounds. Olivia's smile and posture are a mixture of beauty and grace and even though her walk is that of a model, her pose is what portrait's are made from. Olivia has coal black hair which she wears in tiny curls that accents her body's small features quite well. L.T. of course being the gentleman that he is allows Olivia to speak first which she does starting with her name. Olivia then adds, "I'm from Birmingham, Alabama. My father's name is Walter and my mother's name is Susanna and my only brother is named Leon."

Olivia's major is computer programming and she has a 3.47 GPA. She continues by adding, "Both my parents and brother have also finished college so I'm actually continuing the family's tradition." Olivia adds, "Except I choose not to attend Tuskegee mainly because I wanted to travel a little." Olivia's father Walter has a B.A. in business from Tuskegee Institute and is pastor of his own church. He also owns a chain of service stations throughout Alabama. Her mother Susanna has been a real estate broker for over seventeen years and she also graduated from Tuskegee University with a degree in economics. As for Leon, Olivia's older brother, he's also a graduate of Tuskegee. He has a B.A. in business management and now oversees the family business.

L.T. is really taken by Olivia's educated background and mainly by the fact that almost her entire family graduated from Booker T.'s Tuskegee Institute. L.T. begins by telling Olivia his name and those of his parents, sisters and brothers, and also about Ms. Johnson and the

Cromwells. Naturally L.T. informs Olivia of the story regarding his name to which Olivia listens as intensely as L.T. did when Albert first told him the story. As the plane prepares to land, the two discover that they have talked back and forth the entire trip from Boston to Japan.

Once on the ground the two are inseparable—love is certainly in the air. There is a relationship blossoming. Throughout their stay in Japan and Korea and even in Moscow, it is a challenge for the two of them to stop making eyes at one another long enough to take notes about the countries they are visiting. The chemistry between the two is right; they both can feel it, but neither is willing to be the first to admit it. Therefore they simply continue to flirt back and forth as they tour the respective countries.

Once back in Boston while out to dinner, Olivia and L.T. assure one another that they have each others phone numbers and addresses, including those of their parents. The night ends with their first kiss. Today both are flying home for the remainder of the summer. Meanwhile, Judge Cromwell lands L.T. another summer job—this time at a major newspaper company. Everyone back at home is surprised at L.T.'s conversations these days because they're filled with talk about Olivia. Needless to mention everyone is pleased to hear of Olivia but they all are quick to remind L.T. of his goals and purpose for leaving home. L.T. is quick to insure everyone that he hasn't lost focus of his vision nor has he lessened in his pursuit for his education.

This year L.T.'s summer job allows him to float around from day to day. Mondays he works with the printer and observe the printing process. Tuesdays L.T. is allowed to observe the advertising and marketing side of the newspaper, while Wednesdays he's invited to sit in on management briefings. On Thursdays and Fridays L.T. is allowed to travel with a reporter as he collects material and later returns to type and edit the stories for print.

L.T. is very excited about his job which is designed so that he doesn't get bored, but then he can't stopping thinking about Olivia either, something he does everyday. L.T. is romantically involved for the first time ever and it is a feeling that words can not describe. Every time he and Olivia talk on the phone their conversation convinces L.T. more and more that she's the girl for him. By the way tonight before they hung up, L.T. asked Olivia to be his lady which she graciously accepted.

As fall and the school year approaches, L.T. and his parents once again exchange bye-byes as once again its back to Boston. Olivia returns about five days before classes actually start and right away she and L.T. stroll across the campus lawn while holding hands, and sightseeing while taking in an occasional movie also. When a guy is in love, five days can certainly fly by as they now prepare for classes that starts tomorrow.

L.T.'s roommate this year is known by his nickname "Party Animal." His actual name is Tim White. Tim wears his brown hair in a ponytail and he sports a shadow beard look on his face due in part to him spending every minute partying; he says he doesn't have time to both shave and attend class. Tim, who is from California, says he has to keep his tan therefore he's always wearing beach clothes, even in the winter under his overcoat. Upon meeting one another, both L.T. and Tim begin informing one another of their beliefs. Tim suggests to L.T. that he study less and party more, and L.T. suggests to Tim that he party less and study more. However, each says that he is willing to bend since they are going to be roommates for at least a year.

L.T.'s junior year is starting off good because this week he made a break through in the big three professors' classes when he was called upon to answer a few questions in each. He and Olivia don't have any classes together but the two get together about three days a week for a few hours, mostly to study and exchange small talk with an occasional movie or bowling on the weekends.

Both are cautious not to allow their relationship to interfere with their education and of course during any phone call back home both families and friends also remind them of their initial goals. This is evident as the first semester ends and both Olivia and L.T. have respectable 3.59 and a 3.74 grade point averages.

Meanwhile Tim and L.T. continue their tug-of-war about one loosening up and the other tightening up. Nearly three months have passed and the two have grown fond of one another and even admire each other's qualities. Tim is fascinated by L.T.'s name origin and having heard of L.T.'s background he also understands why L.T. does not want him to party so that he loses out on this opportunity of a Harvard degree. Tim tells L.T. that he cannot imagine what he would have become had he came from L.T.'s environment. Tim's major is journalism and he hopes to someday own a major newspaper and magazine publication including a television station. L.T. sees that even though Tim parties hard, afterwards he pulls himself together and gets his work done. Needless to say, L.T. has introduced Tim to Henry and Frank and occasionally they all get together and chat.

The holiday season is upon us once again and L.T. is seeing Olivia off at the airport. He later catches his flight home also. Throughout the holidays, a clever L.T. is able to read between the lines of the conversations of both family and friends and he assures all interested parties that Olivia hasn't made him lose sight of his dreams nor goals even though Olivia and L.T. phone one another daily. Sometimes Tim also calls to chat with L.T. Again this holiday season passes in much the usual manner with the exchanging of gifts and the singing of carols.

Now that it's a new year everyone's back to college to pick up where they left off with studies and classes. Frank and Henry, along with Tim and L.T., are studying together this week because old man Tucker is preparing to give a whopper of a test in his history class. They all attend his class at different hours but the test will still be the same. Needless to mention Olivia and L.T. continue to find reasons to spend quality time together. As the two search for a common ground, Tim has been beating L.T. in one-on-one basketball while L.T. wins in tennis and most of the golf rounds. Tim has also been teaching L.T. the concepts of the stock market, the techniques which his father used to become a self-made millionaire. It is a method Tim's father has used for over twenty-seven years and L.T. is certainly capable of mastering the process, according to Tim.

Finding it hard to break from her track days routine, Olivia continues to workout from time to time. She and L.T., along with Tim and Cindy, occasionally go together as they visit L.T.'s four famous places. As spring break approaches, Olivia informs L.T. that her parents request her presence at home so that they can discuss family business. A somber L.T. understands. Needless to say he doesn't harbor any ill feelings toward her. Upon learning of Olivia's trip home, Tim asks L.T. if he would like to come home with him over the break. Tim has informed his folks all about L.T., and he assures him that he is welcome. L.T. is stunned by the offer, especially since Tim has offered to pay for everything. L.T. gladly accepts.

As the spring approaches, everyone is packing and getting into the mood to go. This Friday Olivia's flight leaves around six p.m. so L.T. escorts her to the airport and after a few tender moments, he sees her off. At approximately seven p.m., Tim and L.T.'s flight departs and immediately after the plane levels off at a cruising altitude Tim orders him and L.T. some drinks. L.T. had no idea that scotch had such a kick before tasting it, but after three he manages to stop. Upon arrival to L.A.'s airport, L.T. is in control of his actions but Tim, on the other hand, can hardly identify Ralph, the family's chauffeur. Nonetheless Tim ask Ralph to show L.T. some sights before taking them home. During the tour around L.A., L.T. is all eyes.

Upon their arrival at Tim's family mansion, L.T. is introduced to Mr. and Mrs. White at which time everyone exchanges small talk involving Tim and his ways. Afterwards L.T. asks if he may call his parents and Olivia. The next morning after breakfast Tim has his folks' Rolls Royce and he and L.T. are cruising the town. Without question L.T. is loving every minute of his California visit. Before too long Mr. White and L.T. have a rather in-depth conversation. During this time L.T. puts his best foot forward and wins him over so much that Mr. White allows him to invest on Wall Street through his broker. L.T. has been following a particular stock according to Tim's advice. Therefore Mr. White says any earnings will be L.T.'s to keep, and they agree to dump it (sell the stock) before the boys go back to school. But first Mr. White loans L.T. one thousand dollars to invest of which L.T. keeps only the earned money if any. Mr. White says it's his way of thanking L.T. for providing Tim with sound guidance and for being one of the few people to be able to get through to Tim regarding sound judgement and decision making.

The following morning Tim and L.T. are up early to eat breakfast and then they're off to the beach where they check into a hotel. Each has his own suite, which leaves L.T. speechless. Naturally Tim is ready to party while L.T. is content with just enjoying the view. Night after night the parties are jumping and Tim is doing his best to make the most of it while L.T. is moving with caution. He could possibly get involved with one of these honeys (girls) if he and Olivia weren't already involved. After a week of partying L.T. goes back to discover that his stock's investment profit is fourteen hundred dollars. Mr. White quickly informs L.T. that stocks are funny, in that an investor must know when to buy and when to sell and to never get excited about stocks. Mr. White then writes and gives L.T. a check for fourteen hundred dollars.

It certainly turned out to be a spring break and an over-all learning experience that L.T. will never forget. Overall the boys had a memorable time and the Whites will never forget L.T. and his mannerisms. During the flight back to Boston's Logan airport the two again toast the scotch and upon arrival L.T. is the man in charge as Tim is stagger-ing as he walks. Once back on campus L.T. puts Tim to bed and quickly runs over to Olivia's room where the two exchange their spring break events before bedtime and the resuming of classes.

Today classes resume and so too the sleepless nights. L.T. has really gotten the hang of Professors Spelman's, Thorpe's and Webster's classes and test materials. As a matter of fact, he is becoming one of their most memorable students. With the passing of each week, school is slowly winding down and summer is fast approaching. Therefore Olivia and L.T. have begun discussing their summer visi-tation arrangements. They have agreed to meet one another's parents. They will go home for the first month and then L.T. will fly to Alabama and meet Olivia's folks and attend the Robinson's family reunion. Afterwards he and Olivia will fly up to New York together where she will met L.T.'s family and friends. Then the two will return to Boston from New York. The last week passes in a blink and before anyone realizes it, school is out for the sum-mer. Both L.T. and Olivia have finalized their plans and are now telling jokes in a taxi cab on their way to the air-port. After checking in their baggage at the airport ticket counters, the lovebirds spend time whispering sweet noth-ings into one another's ears until the time they are to board their respective flights.

9 *FRUITS OF LABOR*

Heritage is very important as a source of inner strength. L.T. is a black man in pursuit of wholesome yet tangible prosperity. If that seems like an insignificant admission, you try saying it. Then, stand back. Raised eyebrows, snickers, scowls and disparaging words will be heaped upon you. Nonetheless he is used to it. Besides, he belongs to a group that, in the eyes of many others, are inferiors who are to be taken lightly, if at all. Stated simply, the quest to succeed has become his reward. In spite of the tarnished perceptions that blacks must occasionally dispel, L.T. remains determined not to slip into the pitfall of mortal men as stated by a noted pastor who describes that pitfall in such a manner: "A man who allows unwarranted perception to govern his actions will make the most detrimental mistake that a melancholy man can possibly make. For someone who isolates himself in a corner, sits down and broods, surfacing his idiosyncrasies, thereby exaggerating and distorting the proportion of truth while by himself, is likely to hear his own despair."

Upon L.T.'s approach down the terminal runway and into Thelma's sight she lets out one of her patented screams before hugging and slapping him on his back. Albert is also moved to do more than merely shake L.T.'s hand so he pulls L.T. into a bear hug. Meanwhile Ms. Johnson stands back awaiting her turn and when it arrives she too almost squeezes the life out of L.T. in her moment of sheer happiness. Ms. Johnson is as proud of L.T. as Thelma and Albert are. Having completed their greetings, the party manages to locate the baggage claim area where they claim L.T.'s luggage. Afterwards, they exit the airport and get into Ms. Johnson's car.

During the drive home Thelma, Ms. Johnson, and occasionally Albert take turns questioning L.T. and commenting on his appearance. At this time L.T. stands approximately 6 feet tall and weights 150 pounds and his blue jeans and pullover shirt fit him neatly. There is a noticeable change in L.T.'s eloquent voice and conversation in general, which of course, are for the better. Upon their arrival to the house, L.T. is surprised at how much his little sister and brother have grown. Pam and Toby, who resemble bean stalks, hug L.T. and proceed to literally talk his ears off. Nearly two hours later, L.T. has finally gotten a chance to show the family and Ms. Johnson some pictures of Olivia. As everyone looks at the pictures, they examine Olivia's features. L.T. answers their questions in the process, reassuring everyone that he is still committed to completing his education. As everyone admires the pictures, L.T. informs them of his and Olivia's plans to visit one another's families during the summer months. This news prompts excitement from everyone.

L.T. then excuses himself so that he may phone the Cromwells whom he chats with for a while before calling Olivia and talking with her and her parents. Olivia then talks with the Thompsons and Ms. Johnson. Shortly after Ms. Johnson's departure, L.T. decides that it is time he shower and turn in for the night.

The first morning home from school in five months is like a dream to L.T. as he awakens to smell the aroma from Thelma's breakfast. So without hesitation L.T. gets out of bed and washes up and hurries on into the kitchen where he and Thelma sit down to breakfast along with Pam and Toby. Afterwards L.T. decides its time to visit the Cromwells and some old friends, including a few memorable places like the Schomburg Center and Central Park among others.

The substation brings back fond memories and so does the train ride leading into the Cromwells community. Upon L.T.'s arrival at the Cromwells he is greeted with hugs, kisses and hand shakes. Everyone quickly moves into the sitting room where they begin to chat, attempting to catch up on all of the happenings that have taken place over the past five months. Judge Cromwell is pleased to see that L.T. has matured in so many different ways yet he still displays that "bulldog tenacity" for learning. Mrs. Cromwell is also pleased to see that L.T. has turned out to be the gentleman she had envisioned years ago. After spending some time with the Cromwells, including Vanessa and Charles, L.T. is off to visit Mrs. Hepburn and others.

Soon after he arrives into the old neighborhood, L.T. quickly notices that the numerous changes have been for the worst. A brief tour is enough to convince him that you can't go back to yesterday. Therefore, L.T. exits the old neighborhood in a hurry. The summer days are as hot as usual with the temperature deadlocked in the low 90's.

Having been home for about five days, L.T. feels it is time he and Ms. Johnson resume their heart to heart discussions regarding his future. It is worth noting that Ms. Johnson is glad to hear from L.T. once again that he and Olivia aren't anticipating marriage or children before graduation. Ms. Johnson has stood steadfast behind L.T. and wants nothing short of success to come his way. The two of them talk for hours whereby they rekindle their friendship and bond to success.

Today L.T. is en route to meet Olivia's family and attend the Robinson's family reunion in Alabama. The flight down to Birmingham is smooth, not much turbulence and the landing is perfect. Once through the terminal, Olivia spots L.T. right away and quickly ushers her parents over to meet him. They all exchange greetings and then claim L.T.'s luggage from the baggage area. One after another, the family members get L.T.'s attention and question him. Each of L.T.'s replies are followed by the proper response— yes ma'am, no sir etc. Naturally L.T.'s mannerisms win over the Robinsons right away. Once at the Robinsons home from the minute they meet, L.T. and Leon seem to get along.

After having gotten settled in including having phoned home, everyone now sits in the family room. L.T. finally gives in to his desire to question Leon and Mr. Robinson in regards to attending Tuskegee. The three of them talk for hours as L.T. asks what seems to be a hundred questions about Tuskegee and its functions. Everyone of his questions is answered in detail by either Leon or Mr. Robinson and they in turn inquire about Harvard which L.T. is glad to discuss. Afterwards Olivia rides L.T. around town and introduces him to some of her friends and they visit some of her memorable childhood places.

L.T. and the Robinsons grow closer with each passing day. As other family members begin to arrive for the family reunion, Olivia makes sure that everyone is introduced to L.T. and he to them. L.T. likes the scenery of the south better than he thought he would. As a matter of fact, he would not mind living in the area someday. Throughout the festivities, Olivia and L.T. are inseparable and most of the older family members are willing to bet that they are contemplating marriage. Mr. and Mrs. Robinson have a feeling that it's just a matter of time before their daughter and L.T. are married, mainly because of the way the two of them stare at one another all hours of the day; its no secret that they are in love.

By and by L.T.'s allotted time draws near to a close. Meanwhile Olivia prepares to visit Albert and Thelma. On this seasonable summer Friday as Olivia and L.T. are driven to the airport by the Robinsons, everyone is certain they'll see each other again. Even though the lovebirds return to school after they spend the upcoming two weeks in New York, the scene at the airport is one of mixed emotions as Susanna and Olivia get a little teary eyed but both manage not to cry, at least not before take off of the flight. Meanwhile Walter assures L.T. that he hasn't ever before taken to anyone like he has to L.T. and Leon assures L.T. that's a fact. Suddenly the final call for Olivia and L.T.'s flight is announced over the PA system and the two of them go aboard the airplane.

As the plane begins its descent and taxis onto the Kennedy runway, Olivia looks into her compact mirror. L.T. assures her she looks fine before they prepare to exit the airplane. Once off the airplane, Thelma quickly spots the two of them and right away she falls in love with Olivia. Albert too gives his approval as both parties exchange bear hugs before moving onto the baggage terminal where they claim the luggage and locate the car. Thelma and Olivia seem to have hit it off from the start as they talk nonstop. Albert has hardly been able to get in a word edgewise before they arrive home and unload the car. Thelma quickly shows Olivia to her room and shortly afterwards they all gather in the family room where they continue to get acquainted.

Shortly after the conversation begins Ms. Johnson arrives and she and Olivia exchange greetings. Afterwards the two of them begin to get acquainted also. Before long the entire family is in the family room where everyone seems to be talking all at once. L.T. manages to slip away to the kitchen where he phones the Cromwells to inform them that he and Olivia will be over to visit tomorrow much to their delight. Nearly some three and a half hours later, Ms. Johnson departs because it is getting late and slowly everyone prepares for bed and a good night's sleep.

The following morning Thelma wakes everyone with the smell of her bacon and eggs along with pancakes and before too long everyone is in the kitchen at the table eating breakfast. Afterwards Olivia offers to assist with the clean up but Thelma will hear nothing about it. Olivia and L.T. then get dressed and catch the subway during which time L.T. informs Olivia all about the subway's history and some memorable moments from a few of his trips. At the Cromwells, Olivia and L.T. are again greeted with bear hugs and kisses as everyone exchanges greetings. Then they sit in the sitting room where they begin to get acquainted. Mrs. Cromwell and Olivia seem to get along from the very start and the Judge and Vanessa admire Olivia's personality.

After nearly three hours, Olivia and L.T. leave the Cromwells but assure them that they will return before the two leave for school. L.T. and Olivia then visit some of L.T.'s old hangouts and memorable places as they stroll along holding hands. Naturally L.T. informs Olivia of all the events that have occurred at the various places and she takes in every word to memory. Day after day Olivia and L.T. are up, dressed and gone sightseeing almost before Thelma can see them, much less feed them. Olivia assures Thelma that it has nothing to do with them not wanting to eat but is due to the fact that she has never visited the city, therefore L.T. is doing his best to insure that Olivia gets to see as much of New York as possible—

Central Park, the Statue of Liberty, Apollo Theater, Broadway and much more. Olivia can't believe her eyes as she take pictures of these landmarks that she has only read about.

L.T. does manage to return a visit to Ms. Johnson at which time Ms. Johnson again reminds him of his life's goals: even though Olivia is a good girl graduation is of the utmost importance. Again L.T. assures her that he and Olivia will complete this last year of college before any distractions become too large to ignore. Ms. Johnson is glad to be reassured by L.T. that he's still committed to completing his education. On this particular Saturday as L.T. is being cross-examined in regards to his future by the Cromwells, Thelma and Pam show Olivia around town.

During this delicate moment in time this phrase by a noted black leader serves as an excellent indication of L.T.'s potential: "A good test for deciding the soundness of any moral stand which a man has taken is the amount of opposition it excites." Following his departure from the Cromwells, L.T. decides to surprise Thelma with a new microwave oven and refrigerator for his parents thirty-fifth wedding anniversary. Therefore he stops by Montgomery Ward where he has placed the items on lay-a-way. Today he is back to pay off the balance and confirm delivery. As he walks through the appliance department, L.T. locates the customer service section where he promptly pays off the remaining amount. The saleswoman proceeds over to a cash register and stamps L.T.'s receipt paid. She then places the money into the drawer. Afterwards she begins to walk away from a baffled L.T. who questions her about delivery procedures at which time the saleswoman simply ignores him as if though L.T. doesn't exist. This is evident in the fact that she continues to entertain other customers. Needless to say such action by her agitates L.T. but not so much that it hinders his ability to address the present dilemma. Therefore L.T. makes certain to obtain his stamped receipt and inquires, "Even though I've spent over one thousand five hundred dollars it doesn't entitle me to all of the services afforded everyone else who spends that much?" This statement does not move the saleswoman who merely turns away from L.T. as if he isn't speaking to her. Without another comment, L.T. proceeds to the front of the store where he requests to speak with the manager. Immediately the representative notices the determined tone of his voice and L.T.'s mannerism which translates into a certain sense of urgency. Shortly after the representative reappears, the manager exits his office and immediately L.T. discovers that the manager is determined to satisfy his demands. Upon completion of L.T.'s explanation, the manager proceeds to the appliance department where he directs the head of the department to make certain that L.T. is adequately served. He then returns to the lay-a-way department and promptly fires the saleswoman. Meanwhile another clerk gathers the required delivery information and assures L.T. that his items will be delivered.

On the following day and at the time agreed upon, Thelma's anniversary gifts are delivered both to her surprise and delight. Now all of the visiting and reassurance are complete pertaining to the two of them completing their education. Tomorrow L.T. and Olivia return to college. Ms. Johnson, the Thompsons, and the Cromwells adore Olivia and everyone hopes to see her again at their graduation if not sooner.

Ring-a-ding! The alarm sounds but L.T. and Olivia are already up and dressed. So too are Thelma and Albert. After breakfast, coffee and some conversation, they're off to the airport because the flight leaves at nine a.m. At the airport everyone is caught up in looking forward to seeing one another again so much that the last boarding call is announced before anyone takes the PA announcements seriously. Thelma can't help but become misty-eyed as L.T. and Olivia disappear down the terminal towards the airplane. Thelma insists they stay until the plane is airborne.

Naturally Albert refuses to argue over the issue. Having watched the plane for as long as possible without uttering a sound, Thelma walks slowly towards the exit. As she walks Albert grabs a hold of her hand and assures her L.T. will be alright.

Immediately upon their arrival on campus Olivia and L.T. put on their thinking caps and begin preparations for the start of school. First they locate one another's dorm rooms and then call home to inform their parents all is well. Afterwards they continue gearing up for school. This year L.T.'s roommate is one of the few black seniors on campus. His name is Arthur Reeves. The two of them introduce themselves and the introduction is nonchalant because they have heard about one another. It must be noted that it seems as if their personalities are going to clash from time to time during the course of this upcoming year. Nonetheless the two of them continue to fix up their sides of the room.

Time seems to pass quicker than normal perhaps because tomorrow is the first day of classes for the seniors, juniors and sophomores; introduction started a week ago for the freshman. Now that the two of them have gotten into their daily routine, time continues to drive a wedge between L.T. and Arthur's relationship. Meanwhile, Olivia and L.T.'s love grows deeper and for the first time ever the topic of marriage is being discussed among them. But due to his election as minority spokesperson along with working part time, L.T.'s schedule is full. Arthur still doesn't offer any assistance or seem to want to totally commit himself to a full fledged friendship, therefore the two of them continue to simply stay out of one another's way.

This year the cold New England seems to be colder than usual. Winter has brought with it what seems to be tons of snow; nonetheless the holiday season is a welcome sight. After riding to the airport in a horse-drawn carriage L.T. sees Olivia's plane off; about forty-five minutes later he catches his flight out for home. This Christmas is one of reunion for the Thompson family; Muhammad and Sara are home along with L.T. for the first time in four years. Its seems that everyone is doing quite well for themselves and they are looking forward to the coming year. There are all sorts of storytelling along with recollections of past events told by everyone. The Christmas dinner is prepared by Sara and Pam while Thelma simply sits at the table and coaches the girls through preparations of various dishes. Meanwhile in the family room Albert and Toby join L.T. and Muhammad in a sort of round table discussion regarding the plight of black men.

The tree has more presents under it than ever before and on Christmas morning the living room looks like a hurricane hit it after everyone has opened their presents. As the family sits down to dinner it brings back fond memories of the past as everyone takes turns recalling their most memorable events. My how time flies when you're having fun. Before long it is time to bid one another farewell. L.T. is the first to leave, followed by Sara then Muhammad. Needless to say, Thelma cries upon each departure.

Immediately upon arrival at school, Olivia and L.T. are wrapped up in one another's arms, exchanging holiday details among other things. However, it isn't long before classes break the routine of sleeping late and also bring with them the demand for study time. As the trees begin to sprout blooms once again, it is time for spring break and everyone is packing and getting ready to have some fun. That is, everyone except L.T. who is on his way to a small Florida town for recognition day to be held in his honor. He and Professor Thorpe are on their way to Clermont, Florida. Clermont is a small town in central Florida, located about twenty miles west of Orlando. About three months ago, Professor Thorpe's brother-in-law ,who is the head of Clermont's Chamber of Commerce committee, spoke during a phone conversation one night to the professor about the city's lack of proper street lighting and the need to repair some roads. At that time Jim stated that the city needed approximately a million dollars in order to have streets, parking lots, and parks properly lit after dark, and make road repairs. "But the town can't afford any more debts at this time," he added.

In an attempt to solicit some assistance, Professor Thorpe did not say anything to his classes, but one Thursday morning he did write in the lower left hand of the blackboard a brief summary about Clermont's lighting and roads situation. The professor's note read, "As a volunteer project the city of Clermont, Florida has a street lighting and road repair problem which they need to have resolved. However, the town doesn't have any money to fund the project. Send a suggestion to the town's folk if you're concerned." Professor Thorpe left the note on the board only for one day.

L.T. accepted the challenge and devised a plan for the town of Clermont. He wasn't the only student to send in a suggestion, but his suggestion was chosen the winner. L.T.'s plan went something like this: first of all, from a combination of his own stock investments and donations from friends and acquaintances he contributed fifteen hundred dollars to Clermont's deficit. Then L.T. suggested, in order for the citizens to raise the remaining amount, the city's power and light company, all major grocery stores, telephone company, service stations, and the cable company must assist. They must agree somewhat along these lines: since these establishments provide the town's folk with needed services, people feel compelled to pay for their services. Therefore, L.T.'s plan called for all of the mentioned businesses to provide service totalling the amount that people donate (ranging between five to twenty-five dollars) to the chamber of commerce. For example, if a customer donates five dollars and has a receipt from the committee and takes that receipt into the telephone company, then the phone company would collect the receipt and deduct five dollars from his bill. In addition, a five cents tariff is to be put on all required functions such as preparation of all official documents and a twenty-five cents hike on all parking meters will be added. In addition, churches and other civic organizations such as VFW'S, Messianic's, and local clubs will be charged an additional hundred and fifty dollar operation fee every ninety days until the targeted amount is raised. This practice including various fund raisers will be staged until the amount is collected. Afterwards businesses will return to normal operations.

Today at Boston's Logan airport, Olivia and L.T. exchange farewells with the understanding that Olivia will meet L.T. and Professor Thorpe in Clermont once she has visited with her folks. Besides since they are engaged, they need to look for a potential home town. Professor Thorpe paid for L.T.'s round trip flight. During their flight, the two become somewhat close, especially after L.T. enlightens the professor as to the origins of his name.

Upon arrival in Clermont, L.T.'s somewhat upset because his mind is on his lost luggage. Besides this small town atmosphere doesn't really interest him. But, nonetheless being the gentleman that he is, L.T. cruises around town with the Professor and Bill as they view the sights. Afterwards L.T. returns to his hotel where he changes into his newly purchased pajamas and robe after dinner and sits out on the deck to observe the scenery. Night has fallen on Clermont and the moonlight transmits a romantic reflection as it illuminates the lake that catches L.T. eye while he rocks back and forth in the rocking chair. The scene provides a soothing calm that causes L.T. to nod off before he gets up and beds down for the night. The morning doesn't bring any good news regarding L.T.'s luggage as he discovers that it won't be until tomorrow that his bags will arrive.

Nonetheless L.T. rents a car and picks up Olivia from the Orlando airport and the two sightsee around central

Florida for the remainder of the day. Thanks to Olivia's map-reading abilities, the two arrive in Clermont at dusk and the sunset is the most beautiful sight that either has ever witnessed. L.T. and Olivia stop by the hotel where L.T. phones Bill to inform them that they are okay. After a shower and change of clothes, L.T. and Olivia take in Clermont's night life which turns out to be just what the doctor ordered. The activities happens to be simple which suits both L.T. and Olivia just fine so they down right like the little place. Since it is within driving distance to some larger cities, they admit that the little town could possible grow on them. Besides it seems to be somewhat lucky for L.T. However, they also keep open the possibility that they could move after a year or two if things did not work out. Promptly at seven a.m a knock is at the door. It is the airline baggage handlers with L.T.'s bags.

A relieved L.T. dresses for the ceremony to be held in his honor. It takes place on the town's City Hall steps where the mayor presents L.T. with the key to the city. L.T. graciously accepts and says a short speech and the program ends. Afterwards L.T. informs Professor Thorpe that he will fly back to Boston from Birmingham with Olivia and that if there is any difference involving his ticket he will pay it himself. Upon hearing this, Professor Thorpe decides to stay at Jim's place another day longer. The two then go their separate ways.

Upon L.T. and Olivia's arrival at the Robinson's home, while looking at the pictures from the City Hall ceremony, Olivia informs her parents of their decision to get married and live in Clermont after graduation. The statement "after graduation" brings relief to Walter's heart. However, the news is much to the Robinsons delight. L.T. then phones his parents and informs them of the news. A slightly disappointed Thelma had hoped they would live closer but understands why they chose Clermont. But overall she is pleased to hear the news and is looking forward to having Olivia as a daughter-in-law. Ms. Johnson is also both glad and sad; glad they decided to graduate first, yet sad that the couple has chosen to live so far away. Nonetheless she's proud of the fact that L.T. can make the hard decisions of life with confidence. Mixed emotions are again felt by the Cromwells in that they too had hoped for L.T. to live closer but the news was good to hear. Judge Cromwell rationalized that L.T. and Olivia need to put down their own roots and that sometimes the best way to do that is away from family.

Once he's back to school from spring break, L.T. proudly shows off the ceremonial pictures to everyone in between class, including Arthur. With the school year fast coming to a close, L.T. and Arthur still haven't quite come to terms as true friends. Neither disrespect the other nor does one go out of his way to help the other either, perhaps its jealousy. It must be noted that jealousy is defined as, "Fearful or wary of being replaced by a rival, arising from feelings of envy, apprehension, or bitterness."

On this the first of May, inside the professors lounge Professors Thorpe, Spelman and Webster are all discussing L.T.'s character and potential, and all are in agreement that only the sky can limit his achievements. Today May 3rd L.T. is celebrating his twenty-first birthday and just as important to him, today marks three years that he has been a registered voter. Olivia has organized a get together with all of her and L.T.'s roommates over the past four years to celebrate L.T.'s birthday. All are in attendance except for Arthur who says he has to study. Nearly two hours into the celebration, Tim proposes a toast which everyone joins. Afterwards L.T. asks that one by one everyone stand up and share their future plans. Well after a few drinks some wild futures lie ahead. But through it all the celebration turns out to be a success and all is well that ends well.

Now as graduation week approaches, L.T. and Olivia have agreed to get married exactly one week after graduation in New York. This date and location allows for many of their classmates to attend and it's no problem for the Robinsons to fly up from Alabama. Meanwhile Thelma, Susanna, and Ms. Johnson along with Mrs. Cromwell have been busy for weeks making and completing the preparations. The wedding will take place in Rev. T. L. Brown's church in Harlem with Rev. Brown preceding and Olivia's father will give her away. But as for now, first matters first, which is graduation day at Harvard.

It seems as if though the entire Thompson and Robinson families have made the trip to Boston for this memorable day. There are more family members present than there were at the last family reunions. Needless to say, they all are seated together, along with Ms. Johnson, the Cromwells, Vanessa and Charles as well as families members who haven't been seen in over ten years. But then after all, this is graduation day.

After the guest speaker, who happens to be the President of the United States, finishes his speech the diplomas are awarded. Olivia's name is called before L.T.'s. Afterwards everyone in the party applauds and is cheering as loud as they possible can! Everyone except Susanna, who can't help but cry tears of joy as her baby's name is announced. Walter, who is a little choked up himself, comforts Susanna who quickly regains her composure. Nearly twenty minutes later the name Luther Taliaferro Thompson is announced and just as if they had planned it Thelma, Ms. Johnson, Carolyn and even Mrs. Hepburn break down crying tears of joy. Meanwhile everyone else cheers and applauds as loud and as hard as they possible can. Before too long everyone regains their composure. Finally the ceremony ends and the family members quickly make their way down to congratulate the graduates.

After everyone is finally loaded into the various automobiles, the drive back to Harlem is filled with gala conversation and best wishes occasionally mixed with tears of happiness. Arrival in Harlem takes on new meaning—preparation for the wedding. Last minute checks are being made on everything from the church reservations right down to the shoes L.T. is to wear. This week L.T. is having discussions almost daily with Albert, Judge Cromwell, and of course Ms. Johnson after Thelma releases him. Reality has long set in on L.T. that marriage is a big deal, and these conversations are reinforcing such a decision.

Today Ms. Johnson informs L.T. of the story she tells all her students about him and his trials. She assures him that if he continues to work as he has that he will clear any hurdle regardless of the height. On L.T.'s final visit to the Cromwells, the Judge lets him in on a little secret, telling L.T. that he is the only person to have read every single book in his library. L.T. replies, "I needed every bit of information in each book in order to get through school." Judge Cromwell leads everyone in laughter after L.T.'s reply.

Another memorable day in the life of both Olivia and L.T. is here which happens to be their wedding day. Family members and friends are gathering fast it appears that approximately a hundred and thirty-four guests are in attendance. The decorations within the church are gorgeous and a four layer wedding cake that is pink with blue roses is in the reception room. There is also a white limo parked outside with a chauffeur waiting to sweep the bride and groom away after the ceremonies. At the present moment, Rev. Brown has positioned himself at the altar steps and the organ begins to play. Meanwhile Leon and numerous other family members have their video cameras rolling.

L.T., who's decked out in a white tuxedo with small gray pinstripes and is trimmed in gray, awaits Walter and Olivia who are slowly marching down the aisle. Olivia's gown is pearly white and the six foot train is speckled with pearls. Her veil is also accented with pearls. Once Olivia and Walter arrive at the altar, the musician softly plays the love song, "When we get Married" as the wedding vows are exchanged, ending with the traditional kiss. Olivia and L.T. exit the church amidst the traditional rice throwing. They reappear at the reception where they conduct the cake-cutting ceremony. The couple then dance their first dance as husband and wife. Afterwards the two mingle with their guests, before dashing off to their honeymoon in the Caribbean.

Oh! The clear blue water is a beautiful sight and it's so romantic. Olivia and L.T. fool around in the water on their first day as Mr. and Mrs. Luther Thompson while the Caribbean serves as a lovely backdrop. Olivia must do her womanly duties daily, that is to go shopping, while L.T. snaps pictures as they roam the streets semi-looking for bargains but mainly holding hands and kissing. By night the couple dance under the colorful sky around the campfire along with the native residents to various Caribbean sounds. After seven days on different islands, the time has come for the couple to return to the States and set up house.

Olivia and L.T.'s plan calls for Olivia's earnings to pay the bills while L.T. concentrates on law school and passing the bar exam while studying the stock market as well. It should be noted that L.T. and Olivia arrive in Clermont far better off than many newlyweds. Both drive a new Honda Accord equipped with telephones given to them as wedding presents and neither has to pay off any school loans and thanks to L.T.'s Wall Street investments they have nearly thirty thousand dollars in their bank account. Olivia has already been hired at Walt Disney World movie studios teaching computer programming and special effects. L.T. will attend the University of Florida Law School at its Orlando based branch.

Day by day the newlyweds complete one task after another regarding getting settled into their new three bedroom, two car garage gray brick home located in the middle class section of town. The town folks are so friendly and helpful too as L.T. and Olivia continue to learn their way around including the main routes leading to some of the surrounding cities like Orlando, Lakeland, Daytona Beach, and Tampa just to name a few. As Florida's hot summer days introduce themselves to the newlyweds, both agree that it will take some getting used to.

As expected L.T. and Olivia join all of the town's committees they possible can; NAACP, Chamber of Commerce, they even obtain exception to policy in order to join the PTA so that they might have a voice during times that require suggestions for the improvement of Clermont's schools. L.T.'s schedule reads Monday, Wednesday, and Friday he attends classes, obtains information and suggestions, etc. while Tuesdays and Thursdays are split between working with a local law firm and investing in the stock market. Olivia's schedule varies. However, she normally arrives to work around nine thirty a.m. and departs around four thirty p.m., but when a movie is in production her schedule changes according to shooting times. The initial work week is full of learning experiences for both the Thompsons but as time progresses, they begin to catch the hang of things. L.T. still studies like a man possessed so that he might pass the bar exam the first time around.

Needless to say the Thompsons social calendar has very few dates but they do manage to attend many of the PTA meetings and numerous other township meetings also. Between all of the requirements L.T. studies for the bar exam and he has also made a few rewarding investments on Wall Street. The phone calls to and from the parents happens weekly but those from old friends don't come as often as they once did. But when one does come, its greeted with excitement. As the months begin to amount to one year, then another and before too long the Thompsons are about to begin their third year in Clermont. Over the years Olivia and L.T. have continued to exercise at the gym, attend church, maintain their bank account, and read from various libraries. Sandwiched between those years L.T. has managed to get elected to a city council seat and in approximately three weeks he is going to take the bar examination for the first time.

10 *DRIVEN BY IMAGES*

At this point there are a few questions that should be asked: first of all, why is it so hard for us, the offspring of slaves, to adhere to the guidelines for global survival (ie, education is power, good things don't come easy) that our parents stress so hard upon us? Secondly, why must we, the offspring of slaves, find it so hard to believe someone (our elders in particular) when they inform us of the hardships that are lying at the end of the road upon which we are presently traveling, when we know that they have encountered the potholes along this same road? Thirdly, at what point in time during our existence will African-Americans truly grasp the concept pertaining to success in that if we pull for one another then we can make it, she

can make it, he can make it, you can make it and therefore,
I can make it? Finally, when are we African-Americans
going to realize that the road to success is accessible via
numerous paths?

After sixteen long hard years of studying and trying to
walk the straight and narrow path that leads to success,
L.T. now sits in the lounge of the Orlando Florida Federal
Building along with some two hundred others awaiting the
computer-graded results of his bar examination. As he
waits for a moment L.T. thinks of how he will break the
news to Olivia if he doesn't pass but then his mind doesn't
allow him to dwell on the negative. Suddenly one of the
test administrators enters the lounge with the results and
announces, "If I call your name please follow me after the
last name has been called. And if your name isn't called
you will receive information regarding retesting in about
one month." The first name called is Luther Thompson.
L.T.'s heart literally turns a flip within his chest. The administrator continues down the list until the last person's
name is announced. Those whose names were called then
follow the administrator down the hall congratulating one
another along the way. Once inside the huge ceremony
room. Everyone is asked to stand and take the oath required in order to become lawyers. Afterwards everyone
lets out various sighs of relief and then they all make their
way through the exits to share the news with loved ones.

Upon L.T.'s arrival home, the smile on his face tells
Olivia that he has passed even before L.T. actually speaks.
Olivia quickly runs into the kitchen to get the bottle of
champagne she has had chilling on ice since early this
morning. She quickly pops the cork, then fills two chilled
glasses. The couple then makes a toast to everyone who
helped to make this day possible. Having consummated
L.T.'s status as lawyer, they emerge from the bedroom.
Afterwards Olivia gets their personal phone book and dials the Thompsons whom they inform. Then they phone
the Robinsons, Ms. Johnson, the Cromwells, they even

phone Tim White and other college classmates before they are done for the night.

One week after passing the bar exam, L.T. is hired by the Nagel Law Firm he has worked for over the past three years. On the political front he has been elected to a seat on the city council for a second term. L.T. and Olivia have established themselves as pillars of the community while L.T. continues to make waves with his suggestions and fund raising ideas. By doing so L.T. has put himself into position to become the town's next mayor, if he so desires.

By and by, time passes. In the process L.T. has taken on and won three court cases, nothing really big, and Olivia has received three raises on her job. But today the big news is that L.T.'s Wall Street investments have sky rocketed through the roof, making him and Olivia millionaires. However, the really good news at this time is Olivia is six weeks pregnant. Now that the pregnancy has been confirmed, the Thompsons thumb through their personal phone book as they dial the telephone numbers of both family and friends. The reactions of happiness are the same from both the Robinsons, and Thompsons and including their many friends. As Olivia began to show more noticeably she and L.T. agree that it's now time she quit working, at least until after the baby is born. Then if she wishes to resume her career, she may.

Thanks to L.T. and Olivia, Thelma and Albert now live in a beautiful three bedroom home in suburban New York and Albert drives a Mercedes Benz 450 SEL, and L.T. has also established college funds for Pam and Toby. Thanks to L.T., Sara now owns a small book publishing company in Denver, Colorado while Muhammad has also received financial assistance in funding numerous Nation Of Islam projects. In short, L.T. has displayed the concept of "I've made it, therefore I'm going to assist you in making it also." L.T. and Olivia's new four bedroom four thousand square foot home is completed one month before the baby is due. Their home sits on a hillside overlooking a number of the many lakes that surround Clermont.

Today the ultrasound reveals that the baby is a boy and it appears that all is well. Olivia could have confirmed that all is well due to the amount of kicking and punching that takes place inside her stomach. Both have decided to name their son Malcolm Frederick Thompson after Malcolm X, and Frederick Douglas. Needless to say L.T. came up with the name but Olivia did agree with it. As Olivia's due date approaches Walter and Susanna arrive to be near. They are joined by Albert and Thelma also.

Low and behold, the time has come! Olivia's contractions are four minutes apart so the family is off to the hospital. Upon arrival the staff is prepared and into the delivery room they go. The grandparents prepare to wait in the lounge as L.T. dons his gown and gloves before he joins Olivia in the delivery room. During the delivery L.T., who is taking into account that Walter is a preacher, has no idea that Olivia knew such profanity. Approximately seventeen hours later and like the miracle that usually takes place at birth, Malcolm Frederick Thompson is born. The mother and son hospital stay is brief but once Olivia and Malcolm arrive home, L.T. along with the grandparents take turns spoiling both baby and mom. More importantly, L.T. and Olivia must learn the technique of feeding and handling Malcolm before the grandmothers' departure. Three memorable weeks have passed since Malcolm's birth and the grandparents are leaving the new parents on their own to begin the process of parenting.

Nightly L.T. and Olivia switch off with the feedings and diaper changing as everyone gets accustomed to the routine. With each passing day Malcolm looks more and more like L.T. as he passes through the precious time periods of crawling across the floor, eating in his high chair, and staggering along the furniture while attempting to walk. An examination of L.T.'s political future appears bright as he announces his intentions to run for mayor in the upcoming election.

L.T. has campaigned steadily the past ten months against the likes of four other candidates for mayor. The campaign has been a clean one but it must be noted that L.T. stands head and shoulders above the other candidates, which is proven at the polls where he wins in a land slide.

Some six months later on this wintery overcast morning L.T. awakens and gets out of bed earlier than usual because today is his first official day in office. The morning routine consists of a visit to Malcolm's room. However this morning upon L.T.'s arrival into Malcolm's room, he discovers Malcolm doing one of the two things he does best—sleep; the other is to eat. L.T. then goes into the kitchen and prepares himself some coffee while sitting down at the table to do his usual morning reading and/or studying. He read early in life that Dr. King would get up early and read. Therefore, L.T. does the same each day.

On this particular morning L.T. is finalizing some plans which he intends to introduce to the citizens of Clermont, but first he must put them before the city council members. Having made his way to City Hall and finalized the remodeling of his office, L.T. formalizes himself with some of the duties as mayor. Later in the day during L.T.'s first meeting with the City Council, he opens by informing them, "My methods for producing change will require two very important ingredients. They are unity and dependability." He goes on to express with the utmost importance that assistance will have to come from the business giants, those being the power and light company, banks, large grocery stores etc. L.T. assures the representatives from the noted businesses that their profits will not suffer but before his plan has run its course their earnings are certain to increase. However, L.T. adds, "All of Clermont's citizens will benefit from my plans."

L.T. then opens the floor to comments, recommendations etc. After a brief discussion of various topics, the meeting closes on a positive note. As the following months began to tick off, one community project after another is taken on by City Hall and completed. They are small, but nonetheless the citizens and business community accomplish each task with maximum participation. As Clermont's citizens begin to take pride in their new found political unity, positive fallout sweeps throughout the city. The population begins to grow, not by leaps and bounds but steadily. The local high school wins the state championship in both football and basketball in the same year.

Equally important ,Olivia and L.T. still manage to spend quality time with Malcolm. Two years later Clermont looks noticeably different. Meanwhile construction sites are booming as L.T. introduces the new Clermont to surrounding cities whereby mutual business interests materialize. The advertising drive has really paid off in the way of generating new business and population growth. As for the Thompsons, they continue to attend church, exercise and monitor their portfolio. This summer the family will vacation in Washington D.C. They try to visit a place of learning yearly and there is no better place than the nation's capital.

During telephone conversations with a few of his friends L.T. learns that Tim White has gotten married and has two children. Tim has opened his own newspaper and magazine companies and owns a television station. L.T. also learns that his old roommates Frank and Henry have entered politics. Meanwhile Leon has turned the family's business into one of the top black enterprises in America. On another positive note, Olivia has organized a local group whose aim is to teach slow learning citizens to read, write and perform basic math skills, regardless of their age, race or nationality. Olivia's volunteer group also hopes to introduce basic computer functions to the town's underprivileged citizens. Each week night for two months a term for approximately two hours nightly at the local high school, lives are changed, thanks to Olivia and eleven volunteers.

Just ninety days after Malcolm's third birthday, Olivia gives birth to their lovely daughter whose name is Harriet Sojourner. She's named after the trailblazers Harriet Tubman and Sojourner Truth. It's election time once again for the mayor's office and L.T. has decided to run again—this time against two new opponents. But it's no contest! As L.T. prepares for yet another productive term his law practice is in full bloom as word of mouth has spread regarding the fact that he has yet to lose any of his seventeen cases. Olivia has chosen not to reenter the work force until Harriet Sojourner is at least three years of age.

L.T. is as driven in his second term as he was during his first term. Project after project is discussed, planned, and completed with unexplainable excitement. The citizens of Clermont have developed such wholesome relationships throughout the city's various communities that the atmosphere is almost like that of a fairy tale. Meanwhile L.T. has spent nearly two hundred and fifty thousand dollars of his own money assisting with the completion of a few projects in order to better the city from top to bottom.

On the home front Harriet has passed the high chair and crawling phase too; she is even walking on her own. All of the grandparents make as much of a fuss over her as they do Malcolm. Malcolm and L.T. seem to be working hard to spoil Harriet and Olivia doesn't mind it at all. Watching over the family's portfolio that has surpassed eight million dollars along with keeping an eye on the kids are the primary duties that fill Olivia's days. Nightly Olivia and her fifty volunteers continue to train the city's unskilled citizens.

As he approaches his eighth year in office, L.T.'s ideas and personal commitments have truly revolutionized Clermont's lifestyle. His style of politics has brought in new business, developers, and skilled laborers, which have resulted in a population explosion averaging over fifteen thousand new residents annually. Clermont is climbing in terms of tourist attractions throughout the state.

As the curtain of time is thrown back to reveal a span of twenty years, history notes that ten different teams won the Super Bowl, fifteen different teams claim the NBA Championship, while ten teams took home the World Series title. The business world has changed too numerous to count. Meanwhile all means of transportation are still considered too slow for today's commuters. Fashions have gone out of style and come back into style so often until most people aren't interested in them anymore. The price of major items like a loaf of bread have gone from 25 cents to a $1.75, a pair of tennis shoes have jumped from twenty dollars to eighty dollars, while a gallon of gasoline has gone from 45 cents a gallon to $2.20.

The elder Thompsons are now in their late sixties. Albert has retired and now is occasionally bothered by arthritis in his bad knee but he manages to play hide-and-seek with his grandchildren. As for Thelma, she is still in good health as she attends to her twelve grandchildren with the same passion as she does church matters. Muhammad is married and he and his lovely wife have three children. They call Chicago home where Muhammad is a leader within the Nation of Islam. Sara is also married and has two children. She and her family live in Denver, Colorado where she owns a book publishing agency. As for Pamela, she too is married with two children and works as a disc jockey for one of New York city's leading radio stations. Toby's also married with three children and he's an interstate trucker working for the same union Albert did.

The elder Robinsons are also in their late sixties. Susanna has aged gracefully and if anyone asks how she managed to do so, she credits her four lovely grandchildren. Walter has also slowed down. He has turned over full control of the family's company to Leon— only the welfare of his grandchildren worries him these days. Leon is married to Gail who was Olivia's best friend while growing up. Leon has turned the family's firm into one of the top twenty-five among black businesses in America. Leon is also a member of the Black Business Association Board of Governors.

Ms. Johnson has long hung up teaching and now she just enjoys life one day at a time. Occasionally one of her old students will visit but the conversation usually ends when she talks of L.T. longer than the visitor cares to hear. As for the Cromwells, they spend their time traveling these days. Vanessa and Charles no longer work for them but everyone keeps in touch. L.T. and Olivia are forty-nine years old and both look years younger than their actual age. Malcolm is twenty-five years old. He recently passed the bar examination and is living and practicing law for the NAACP in Alexandria, Virginia. As for Harriet she is twenty-two and has just entered Harvard Law School.

A brief glance at some of L.T.'s old high school and college acquaintances reveals that as for the high school foe Billy Tubbs, he is married, living in Austin and is presently the governor of Texas. Billy has been labeled as an up and coming Democratic presidential candidate. Gail Anderson works as a television news anchorwoman for the leading station in the nation's capital. Gail lives in Washington D.C. with her husband and son. L.T.'s first year roommate at Harvard, Henry Reed, is into politics. He's presently serving his first term as governor of Michigan. Second year roommate Frank Taylor is also into politics and is the newly elected governor of Illinois. Tim "Party Animal" White is the sole owner of the largest newspaper in the nation as well as owner of a magazine and two nationwide television stations in Los Angeles. Now as for Arthur Gibson, he owns his own business in Alexandria, Virginia. He's presently the president of the Black Caucus and is one of the most powerful African-American organizers today. Arthur's humanitarian organization called Attitudes has a membership that averages nearly 57,000 in many of the south, eastern and southeastern states.

Meanwhile back in Clermont as L.T. runs for a seventh term, television cameras are positioned everywhere because his name has surfaced as the top nominee to become Florida's next attorney general. Shortly after winning his seventh term, L.T. is later elected President of the National Conference of Black Mayors. L.T. also holds the titles of President of the National Bar Association, as well as Grand Polemarch of Kappa Alpha Psi Fraternity, and he's also serving his sixth year as President of the National Association for Equal Opportunity in Higher Education. At this year's Black Mayors Convention, L.T. and Olivia are a lovely couple as their arrive in Detroit. L.T. quickly addresses the issues on the agenda. Afterwards the mayors get down to the business of generating workable solutions to the various problems of the inner cities. After a week of decisions to include completion of the election of officials, the mayors adjourn with intentions of presiding over their city's problems in accordance with the ideology discussed during this convention.

Upon L.T. and Olivia's arrival back into Clermont it should be noted that since L.T.'s first election to office over twenty years ago that Clermont's population has grown from nearly 30,000 to over 3,500,000 making Clermont the fasting growing city in the history of the state. Business development and earnings have quadrupled nearly seven times during L.T.'s term in office. Due to all the past accomplishments everyone feels unexplainable joy as they witness renewed hope in the eyes of young and old citizens upon completion of various tasks while L.T. serves as Mayor. Nonetheless L.T. and Olivia have decided that this is L.T.'s last term in office. The political arena has allowed L.T. to fulfill a life long dream in that by practicing the characteristics of his namesakes he has contributed to producing a better city.

On this Friday night while Oprah Winfrey interviews L.T. on another one of her specially televised programs, seated together in Alexandra, Virginia are ten of the most influential black Americans who are part of the television audience. These influential leaders are gathered at the home of Arthur Gibson and they are discussing an "earth shattering possibility." Because L.T. has emerged as one of the most prominent black politicians in the country, along with the fact that L.T. has stated that he will not seek reelection to the Mayorship of Clermont, these gentlemen are assessing L.T.'s potential for the presidency. As the discussion continues among the black leaders, all are not yet convinced that L.T. will be the best candidate for their organization's votes. That is until Oprah asks, "Mayor Thompson, what is your opinion regarding the present situation of blacks in America, and what must they do in order to change the nation's perception of blacks?" L.T.'s response to just such a question might serve as the needed element to convince the four undecided leaders that perhaps he does possess the preparedness required to run for the presidency.

A calm and composed L.T. turned to face the camera then eloquently replied, "The plight of the African-American to simply exist is a rather perplexing dilemma. I say that because of the many variables that must be considered along his journey from his cradle to his grave. Following the birth of each black American it should be noted that the utmost motivating factor for challenging life's journey is acceptance into mainstream society. This society into which he hopes to gain acceptance is not one of a foreign land but it is his birthland that doubles as his homeland. This land I'm referring to is known throughout the world as the land of the free—geographically it is called the United States of America."

L.T. continued adding, "Uncharacteristically woven into the existence of all African-Americans are the terms 'plight' and 'journey.' These terms have a significant place within the lives of America's largest group of minority citizens because of these reasons: first, blacks cannot categorize everyone who is not of African descent as an enemy; secondly, blacks cannot assume that everyone of African descent can be looked upon as an ally. Therefore, the black man must display the character to judge each man, be he black or otherwise, according to the displayed characteristics of the man in his presence." L.T. concluded by saying, "Oprah, such a requirement doesn't provide a quick resolution to the numerous misfortunes that plague black minorities. However, the approach does provide a foundation for building sound judgement whenever one's character must be displayed."

Upon completion of that statement the vote become unanimous among the gathered leaders to approach Clermont's Mayor Luther Thompson and urge him to challenge the Democratic Party for its nomination to run for President. Oprah thanked the Mayor and his wife for the interview but before sounding off the air Oprah asked, "Mr. Mayor are there any announcements that you would like to make regarding your future plans?"

L.T. smiled as he replied, "I can assure you if there were any bombshells, I would disclose them at this time, but I don't have any." The interview ended with a thank you to the sponsors and a goodnight from Oprah.

Two days later a surprised L.T. is stunned to hear his receptionist announce, "Mr. Mayor there is a gentleman here who says he is your old roommate, a Mr. Arthur Gibson, who is requesting to see you."

L.T. quickly states, "Let him in Helen."

Upon Arthur's entrance into L.T.'s office, the two share a laugh and exchange events of the past including speaking of their families. After nearly two hours of remembering the good old days Arthur decides to let L.T. in on the real reason why he has come to visit. But before he begins, Olivia enters and everyone shares a laugh. Arthur then returns to a serious tone as he informs both L.T. and

Olivia the real reason behind his sudden unannounced visit. Arthur says, "L.T., I'm here as spokesman representing nine other prominent black leaders whose decision it is to ask you to consider taking on two tasks. One is that you step up and become the much needed global role model for blacks in America. And secondly, my colleagues and I would like for you to consider running for the Presidency on the upcoming election as a Democrat."

Needless to say upon Arthur's completion both the Thompsons have to gather their feet up under themselves before being able to speak. After a brief moment of silence L.T. speaks, "Performance breakthroughs come from pondering the unthinkable."

An uneasy Arthur asks, "Does that mean you'll do it?"

L.T. replies, "Due to such an immeasurable endorsement ,I feel compelled to run. As a matter of fact I'd be delighted to—of course I'll run." Celebration breaks out among the three before they regain their composure as Arthur phones the others in Alexandria to inform them of the news. Later the three continued to discuss L.T.'s historic decision over dinner before Arthur catches a ten thirty p.m. flight out to Alexandria.

Every waking moment must now be spent organizing staff members, platform agenda, press coverage and all the other particulars required in order to run a successful presidential campaign. After six months of discussion and deliberation including identifying staff members, L.T. is now poised to announce to the public his intention to run in the upcoming Democratic primary. Therefore on the official date to announce one's candidacy, L.T. calls a press conference at City Hall, where he announces his intentions to seek the Democratic nomination for the presidency. Now in the eyes of the nation's general public L.T.'s announcement raises only a few eyebrows. However the day after L.T.'s announcement *America Today* which is the nation's leading newspaper, carries L.T.'s picture on its front page. Needless to say the front page story prompts some nationwide discussion. Nonetheless, his candidacy isn't taken seriously because the nation's political analysts are predicting a two man race, between Texas governor Democrat Billy Tubbs and California's Republican governor David Scott.

All sorts of media coverage from Tim's television station "A2Z" and newspaper staff and hundreds of others are at the Texas State Capital as Billy Tubbs officially announces his intentions to seek the Democratic party's nomination for president. Meanwhile across the western states in California, on the steps of the state's capital, Republican David Scott makes his announcement official, bringing the total number of candidates to eleven— four Republicans and seven Democrats.

Meanwhile at L.T.'s headquarters in Clermont, he and his staff have just completed some issues and counterpoints behind L.T.'s campaign slogan title, "SHATTERING THE MYTHS." L.T. knows that the Democratic trail leading up to the convention will not be easy, therefore he and his staff are planning every move in great depth. L.T. has vowed to include the plight and contributions of every race, creed, and nationality that comprise the nation's population. Being the shrewd organizer that he is, L.T. has a knack for accomplishing the seemingly impossible but he has now taken on a task that could be classified as highly unlikely. "Regardless of the height of the hurdle, one must first clear the obstacle within his mind," is the phrase that best sums up L.T.'s character whenever challenged.

11 *EASY TO DISAGREE WITH, IMPOSSIBLE TO DISREGARD*

At this early juncture in the election as L.T. sits alone in his study he contemplates a number of his dilemmas simultaneously. An examination of L.T.'s plight reveals that in order for him to acquire enough votes, he must convince the majority of registered minorities as well as some white voters that meanings exist for such terms as patriotism, justice, and chameleon other than what both Webster and those the nation's governing body define them as. According to Webster's the terms patriotism, justice and chameleon each have various different definitions.

However, in regards to minorities of color and some whites the meaning of those terms aren't quite the same.

First of all patriotism isn't defined as "love and devotion for one's country" but instead means "accept the status quo." Justice isn't defined as "the principle or ideal of moral rightness: equity" but instead means "it's just not for you." And as for the term chameleon, blacks are never to use that term when speaking of the government's policies to enforce civil rights for the citizens of all nations except their own. L.T. hope and prays that his solution lies in his ability to install in all of America's voters the definition of one particular term— buoyancy meaning "to recover rapidly from setbacks and remain afloat."

Often as I look into the eyes of black children, a reflection is often reflected back that says, "This isn't the way it should be. However, this is the way it has to be." As a perplexed L.T. grapples with the realistic chance of a minority being elected president, present day reality doesn't look promising. The latest census report shows that whites make up over eighty percent of the nation's population and blacks are a distance second with approximately thirteen percent while a collection of other multiethnic races equates to the total percentile. It should be noted that these figures are in no way surprising to L.T. for he knew long before now of the disparity in the population figures.

Nonetheless, L.T.'s main concern is how his campaign can reflect the way a public transit system works. By campaigning in such a manner, L.T. hopes to map out a course and by simply traveling the route, the voters will get on board at the prescribed stops/voting places. Stated simply L.T. wants to campaign by staying focused directly on relevant national issues whereby he creates a one for all candidate, in the process accumulating multiethnic support. But such strategy frightens L.T. because he's afraid that black voters will not see his efforts for what they really are but will possibly see him as a sheep in wolf's clothing or perhaps even refer to him as a chameleon.

Life has many parables but few are more noted than this one: all heroes have flaws—maybe that's what makes them even greater, because they overcame their flaws and became heroes. On the other hand noticeable differences that exist between this nation's governing bodies and its minorities of color must be abolished if America is to remain the world's hero. If America is to avoid a repeat occurrence of those biblical cities Sodom and Gomorrah, then changed hearts must saturate the nation. Neither changed hearts nor the showing of respect should be a problem if justice is allowed to prevail from its screaming chambers—those chambers being the hearts and souls of numerous citizens.

Once the political stomping gets underway L.T. quickly considers costs and travels across the state in a customized bus, starting in major cities like Orlando, Tampa, Miami, and the state's capital, Tallahassee. Due to curiosity people are anxious to see and hear L.T.'s campaign issues and for the most part he is warmly accepted. Before too long L.T. takes his campaign across country where he stands up to the political critics while raising money as well. L.T. stomps across Georgia, Virginia, New Jersey, and New York where in some places he receives rousing ovations. L.T. then swings across Ohio, Michigan, and Illinois.

As his campaign swings out west, L.T. answers some tough questions from the potato farmers in Idaho. He also assures the forest workers in Oregon that he will set up a task force to investigate forestry if elected. California proves to be tough due mostly in part to the fact that Republican David Scott holds a strong grip on the state in the eyes of both Democratic and Republican voters. The state of Texas is also hostile ground because of Democratic opponent Gov. Billy Tubbs reputation with the states voters. Slowly L.T.'s style and charisma begins to make a dent, at least in the Gallup polls where occasionally he's projected as high as second among the Democrats, some distance behind front runner Billy Tubbs. Thus far L.T.'s staff has done a great job in researching the issues that plague the nation, arming L.T. with the data required to put American history in perspective.

Mud slinging and negative political ads enter the Democratic Primary with a bang the day after the first election totals became official in which Billy Tubbs wins and L.T. comes in second in New Hampshire. James Boston, one of the candidates, takes the forefront with a political ad that attacks L.T.'s career. But L.T. and his staff refuse to retaliate, choosing instead to let the voters determine his competence. During an interview L.T.'s senior strategist Patricia Brown says, "The commitment that this staff possesses easily translates into emotional and tireless efforts to put our candidate over the top. The ideology such negative statements attempt to convey will be erased by Mayor Thompson's character and the records he has amassed thus far." Governor Tubbs doesn't jump on the mud sling band wagon but the other candidates take pop shots at L.T.'s lack of political positions.

When asked by reporters in various cases about his political career L.T. replies saying, "I've made the most out of the most noted challenging ventures I've had thus far in my life which were to graduate from Harvard University, pass the bar exam, and serve as mayor of Clermont, Florida." He concludes by saying, "Having done so, I now ask the voters to give me another challenge—being the Democratic nomination." The Democrats campaigns are beginning to shape up as a two man race between L.T. and Texas Governor Billy Tubbs. After thirty states, results are tallied; both candidates are in a virtual dead heat. This remarkable showing by L.T. is expected to fizzle out before the convention which is still a month away. It will be held in New York City. As the political picture stands, Republican David Scott is expected to defeat Billy therefore, analysts are predicting that the Democrats will not jeopardize their slim chance for victory with Mayor Thompson's nomination.

Political analysts across the country agree that California's Republican Governor David Scott has the presidency to win simply by running. David has been elected to and held various political offices for over thirty years, he has been California's governor for the past sixteen years and in addition, he is considered to be one of the most powerful political figures in American history. Therefore, the Democratic party's brain-trust knows full well that even with Texas governor Billy Tubbs, their chance of winning the White House is slim, and even slimmer with any other candidate. Meanwhile on the front line the voters are not assisting the Democrats as they continue to elect Billy in one state and L.T. in the other and with only five states' elections remaining, L.T. actually holds a small percentage points lead.

On L.T.'s home front he and Olivia and the children make it a point to talk daily. Their conversations aren't about anything in particular, they're mainly to massage the family's bond. Olivia has been by L.T.'s side every waking moment possible and when she isn't, she's on the telephone or speaking with reporters and even assisting security with their plans. As for Malcolm Frederick, he's doing his best to register voters across the eastern and southeastern states. As for Harriet Sojourner, she's based in California and along with her aunt Debra in Colorado, the two are participating in voter registration drives across the western part of the country. Muhammad has of course solicited the help of his Muslim associates as they sweep the midwest and northeastern states with voter registration and political education drives.

While traveling back and forth across the country projecting his unique style, L.T. has led voters to believe that they have a new type of politician with him—one who will interject change wherever possible. The television station "A2Z" reporters are reporting that L.T's refreshing style is the springboard that has propelled him into the middle of not only the Democratic primary but perhaps the presidential race itself. But most political analysts warn the Democratic supporters not to be mislead by an up-and-comer instead of standing behind a proven veteran. As the Democratic convention approaches, the lead has been flip-flopping between the two front runners. Needless to say as time becomes rare, both votes and voters become more valuable.

On the eve of the convention, Texas governor Billy Tubbs sits alone pondering how nearly thirty years later, he can clear the Luther Thompson hurdle. As Billy allows his mind to replay the scene that night in Radio City Music Hall, he is prompted to slam down his fist in disgust, as the possibility looms that this time he might not win either. But Billy vows that this time he isn't leaving New York City without a victory. With that thought in mind, he and his family leave for the airport to catch their chartered flight.

Meanwhile at his parent's home in New York, L.T., and Olivia's parent's, along with Ms. Johnson, the Cromwells, a few staff members and a host of others are joyously celebrating. Throughout the house and even on the lawn there are various small groups discussing L.T.'s achievement thus far but keeping in mind he still hasn't won the nomination. L.T.'s promising showing has produced one negative—the need for heightened security as rumors of assassination attempts begin to circulate. But on this night, the eve of the Democratic Convention, there isn't a hint of problems before everyone's departure.

Today there isn't a television or radio station across the nation that isn't discussing the potential outcome of the Democratic Convention and who will most likely be chosen the party's nominee. Most newspapers front pages are carrying the pictures of the two front runners: Texas's Governor Billy Tubbs and Clermont's Mayor Luther Thompson. Reporters blanket the city attempting to catch any possible sign of history in the makings.

Once the convention's proceedings get underway, and the lesser candidates throw their support behind one of the party's two stronger candidates, an earth quake effect is produced and L.T. emerges holding a slight margin over Billy. The Democratic Party's brain-trust has begun thinking the unthinkable—a unified ticket. As soon as the results are made public, strategists from both side begin working around the clock in an attempt to put their man over the top. News wires from every sort of telecommunication ever invented begin transmitting messages across the globe. Meanwhile, at the Party's hotel suite that serves as its headquarters, analysts are frantically compiling data and screening ticket possibilities.

A brief examination of Billy's clout as the party's candidate reveals that being the Governor of Texas and its thirty-two electoral votes means huge clout. Billy did very well in winning big in Texas, New York, Pennsylvania, and New Jersey, totalling 103 electoral votes. But in looking at the presidential race, Republican David Scott's running mate is certain to be New York's governor Republican George Conner. Therefore, the 33 electoral votes New York carries will be lost reducing the potential electoral votes he's subject to carry to 70, regarding the states mentioned.

Examining Mayor Thompson's potential for winning the presidency reveals that he won big in Florida, Michigan, Illinois, Ohio, Massachusetts, and California totalling 152 electoral votes. However looking at the big picture, Republican Scott is certain to carry California and its 54 electoral votes, reducing L.T.'s electoral potential votes to 98. But due to Candidate Thompson's friendship with the powerful governors Henry Reed of Michigan, and Frank Taylor of Illinois and their ties to Buck Washington of Ohio, including his standing among Florida voters, it appears that Thompson is subject to maintain a potential 98 votes. At this time throughout America everyone is conducting their own version of reviews and analyses.

The media led by *America Today* (Tim's newspaper) has created a stir by predicting that L.T. will be the Democratic nominee to face Republican David Scott. After another major newspaper seeking mainly to solicit readers echoes the long shot Thompson story, some Democratic delegates begin to think along the same line. The newspaper stories and predictions aren't without validity because L.T. did arrive at the convention leading by a slim 32 votes over Billy, yet needing 67 more to confirm his nomination. Billy needs 99 votes. Further examination reveals the fact that Mayor Thompson's minority status and the fact that voter registration among all multiethnic groups has gone through the roof could certainly help the party come next November. Also L.T.'s style and charisma has resulted in national attention and creditability to a new look within the political arena which strategists can't ignore.

Regarding Billy's support, the party can't afford to lose his powerful support either. The more the Democratic brain-trust ping-pongs the candidates' potential contributions to the party's goal, the more obvious it appears to have both men form the ticket. However, that in itself still creates a dilemma in deciding which man will be running for president. According to the analysts candidate Thompson's small lead upon arrival doesn't indicate that candidate Tubbs can't obtain the necessary votes to become the party's nominee. Therefore, if the ticket is to appear as the party's brain-trust feels it has to in order to be competitive, then the candidates themselves must make it so. Otherwise either candidate alone literally damages the party's chance at the White House.

Meanwhile due in part to the suggestion of Patricia, L.T.'s senior advisor, to Eric, Billy's senior advisor, members from both sides are discussing uniting the party's ticket. But when the news of suggesting he run as the vice president is brought to Billy, he asks if he can sleep on the decision overnight first. On the other hand when the news of the party's proposed unified ticket is given to L.T., he feels it to be a splendid idea but cautions only if Billy is in total agreement.

Having slept on the thought over night Billy and L.T. meet the following morning after breakfast unbeknownst to the public in a hotel away from the convention site. They mend old fences before Billy agrees to run as L.T.'s vice president. An emotional L.T. replies, "I'm grateful of your support and decision." A curious L.T. then asks, "Why after all these years are you willing to team up with me?"

Billy replies, "Mainly because In God We Trust."

A smiling L.T. adds, "All the way to the White House."

As the two candidates secretly combine forces, back at the convention site the party's leaders are wrapping up a motion to invite the candidates up for a discussion in regards to unifying the ticket. The panel then sends out a message asking Billy to appear before the party's committee to which Billy replies, "Certainly."

However upon his arrival, the panel's members are shocked to see both he and L.T. walk in together. They stop in the center of the room then speak one after another saying, "The Democratic Party's presidential ticket is formed with Luther Thompson as nominee for president and his vice president as Billy Tubbs." Naturally the board members are shocked—actually two of them begin experiencing severe chest pains. But nonetheless the party's speaker calls a press conference for two p.m. eastern time to announce the party's decision to the public.

In the midst of media madness the party's spokesman announces the names and their positions on the official ticket. Upon his completion, shockwaves ripple throughout the country and around the globe. The news prompts tremendous requests for interviews with L.T. and Billy or anyone in position of authority within the party. After brief comments and having answered a few questions, L.T. and Billy, along with family and staff members depart the convention site for a little relaxation before constructing an agenda.

Upon his arrival home, Olivia and all the other family members and friends shower L.T. with hugs and kisses much like the night he won the scholarship contest. Celebration fills the Thompsons home as everyone dances until the break of dawn due to L.T.'s place in America's history as the first black nominated to run for president from a major political party.

Discussions with Olivia, Malcolm and Harriet provide L.T. with unexplainable inspiration. The first issues at hand for the unified team are to establish an agenda that both men will agree upon. However, if at any time an impasse appears, L.T. and his staff will make the final decision. As the real campaigning gets underway L.T. quickly draws up points and issues to be discussed from his slogan. The slogan reads "SHATTERING THE MYTHS" and within his first speech L.T. lets it be known that his slogan and its concept includes the trails of every group of American citizens, regardless of their ethic background. The Thompson camp believes that a key issue in the upcoming election involves getting America's working class, the elderly and multiethnic voters to support the ticket. Therefore, in order to do so L.T. will attempt to assure these classes that his election will equate to the effects of a hammer striking upon the clear as glass enclosed myths our nation has observed for years. As if though these numerous myths associated with the supposed inability of America's natural born minority citizens, and in particular blacks, to duplicate, if not better the feats of our fellow white leaders.

Meanwhile, the Republican Party's convention begins this upcoming Monday in Miami, Florida. All the national news stories begin with Republican David Scott who is 56 years old and is a tall 6'6" man with a medium build and all white hair, and a general distinguished appearance. Scott's family has groomed him for the presidency and is determined to get him elected to the celebrated post of President of the United States at all costs. This is evident in the fact that David's family spent in excess of sixteen million dollars during his election to California's governorship. The Scott's family, actually David's mother Rachel, is so driven to get her son elected that close associates have no doubt that she had something to do with L.T.'s nomination, simply because he appeared to be a lesser opponent.

The Republican Party's convention ends as expected with the nomination of David Scott and his running mate New York's Governor George Conners. The first Gallup poll released shows Scott holding a commanding 21 percentage points advantage if the election was held today. Scott quickly informs the public and press that his slogan reads "MAINTAIN THE AMERICAN WAY" which means to maintain the nation's existing conditions. The intention of Scott and Conners is to appeal to the citizens who have fully exercised their opportunity to experience the American dream.

It must be noted that as in most cases, the Republican candidate Scott doesn't have money problems and has a well-organized staff. When candidate Scott is asked to tell the voters his campaign issues and major goals, he replies saying, "A major issue is to reassess the spending by government on the numerous social programs presently in existence. A major goal is to insure that America's government continues on her present road as the world's leader, while getting the most use from past ideologies." He adds, "In short, if America's political system and methods of operation aren't broken, then don't fix them." Media coverage blankets both candidates as they travel about the country addressing unions, townsfolk, and even big businesses. Month after month the candidates stomp along the campaign trail. Republican Scott does so with killer instinct while Democrat Thompson shrewdly negotiates the political waters.

Behind the scenes L.T. diligently studies the reports on issues plaguing the nation and possible solutions to each as they're reported to him by his staff. L.T.'s efforts are becoming clouded by threats on his life as more security is requested from the FBI. Meanwhile behind the scenes in David's camp, investigations of Democrat Thompson have been in progress since identification of the two candidates six months ago. Today the investigation turns up some evidence that might serve a damaging blow to Mayor Thompson's bid for the presidency. David Scott's detectives have obtained information that indicates candidate Thompson is a criminal running for the highest office in the land. Rumors are circulating that Democratic Thompson was arrested while attending college on charges of breaking and entering, attempted rape, communicating a threat and assault with a deadly weapon. There are additional rumors that Republican Scott, who already holds a 21 points lead, is going to challenge little known Democrat Thompson to a debate at a location of Thompson's choice.

At Republican Scott's next campaign meeting, his top advisor and campaign staff detest the debate thing! Eric Baldwin, Scott's senior strategist asks David to weigh the pros and cons of such an action. He continues saying, "We lead him by over 20 percentage points. The nation's voters still do not know this guy's capabilities, and the arrest charges might blow up in our faces." Eric concludes by informing David, "If this arrest issue doesn't persuade the voters ,we might not be lucky enough to find heavy enough dirt on this guy to use like we did with those governorship candidates."

David lets it be known that he doesn't like the idea of being asked to campaign in a less aggressive manner. Having heard enough from his staff, he leans back in his black high back swivel chair. David then informs his staff of his decision saying, "I'm calling a press conference tomorrow afternoon, one p.m., to challenge Luther Thompson to a debate three weeks from tomorrow, at the site of his choice, so that I can blow that bastard right out of these political waters." David then slowly stands his tall frame up from his chair and begins to literally gaze at each of his campaign members. After a brief pause David says, "Therefore I strongly suggest that you all start working on the vital information required for this upcoming debate." He then walked briskly out of the room!

Naturally David's announcement is covered by a media blitz and later sends reporters dashing to L.T.'s headquarters in Clermont for his response. But before responding, first L.T. meets with Billy and his staff to entertain their points of view. Upon meeting with his staff candidate, Thompson lets it be known right off that he wants to except the challenge. Both Billy and the staff agree that he should. A brief discussion ensues as to where the debate should take place. After some discussion L.T., who can best be described as debonair, stands up and quickly the room becomes silent. L.T. stands six feet four inches tall. He weighs 210 pounds and has a well toned body, with graying hair most noticeably in the temple areas that pays a fitting complement to his very dark skin, such a combination makes him a prominent looking man. His gold-rimmed mildly blue tinted prescription glasses don't hurt his appearance either, nor does the tailoring job of his mostly double-breasted suits.

L.T. speaks his choice location saying, "Washington D.C. at the Ford's Theater." L.T. then informs the staff, "Tomorrow at 10 a.m. the press conference will be held at which time I'll accept the challenge to debate Governor Scott." At 10 a.m. the following day it's standing room only at L.T.'s headquarters when he announces that he accepts the challenge. He then names the host city. L.T. adds, "Besides why should we discuss the fate of the nation's future anywhere else than the nation's capital?"

The question surrounding his arrest charges is poised to Mayor Thompson. He responds by saying, "The unfortunate circumstances related to my incarceration came about solely as a case of mistaken identity. Thanks to the moral courage of a little white girl, I was completely exonerated by the victimized white family." Democrat Thompson concludes by saying, "I would like to go on record stating that this assumption by my opponent will not be retaliated." Following that statement L.T. departs the scene as reporters continue yelling questions. The arrest accusations cost Republican Scott approximately seven percentage points in the polls.

With the debate now just one week away, L.T. and his staff are seated around the oval shaped table in the conference room at his headquarters discussing strategy when suddenly the conference room's double doors swing open and two white men who looks like detectives enter. One is carrying a briefcase and both are holding FBI badges face high. Agent #1 says, "We are Federal Agents here in the interest of the U.S. Government. At this time everyone except candidate Thompson must leave the room." Throughout the room there is a hush while facial expressions range from stunned to horrified. L.T. then calmly signals his staff to leave by nodding his head.

Meanwhile Agent #2 has walked around to the opposite side of the table as Agent #1 stands near the doorway with the briefcase. Patricia slowly walks to the doorway where she turns and ask L.T., "Are you sure you want to be left alone with these creeps?"

L.T. replies, "I'm sure these agents wouldn't harm me. It's okay Patricia." Upon Patricia's departure Agent #1 closes and locks the door. Agent #2 takes a seat to the right of L.T. Agent #1 then places the briefcase on the table and takes a seat to L.T.'s left directly across from Agent #2. Agent #1 pops open the briefcase exposing five million dollars. Then in a deep but low tone of voice says, "This five million dollars is yours, no strings attached, provided you withdraw from the election. Otherwise boy, we can't promise you anything."

A dejected and hurt L.T. eyes one agent and eyes the other with a cutting motion before he looks off in a distant stare. Then in his orator's voice says, "For over forty years...I believed that damn creed...we hold these truths to be self evident...and all that other eloquent bullshit... . Nonetheless, I'm judged by the color of my skin." Afterwards the agents make eye contact with one another, then both smirk and begin to stand up. In the process Agent #2 closes the briefcase. The agents then turn and begin to walk towards the door but before they reach it L.T. stands up and puts his right hand into his pocket. Then while pointing to the briefcase with his left hand he informs the agents, "You can get this now," he then points to a huge window behind him and adds, "Or when it gets to the bottom of this damn window."

Agent #2 places his right hand into his coat and grabs hold of his .357 revolver when suddenly the sound of keys jiggling in the door is heard and the door swings open. Patricia and two building security guards enter at which time Patricia says, "I've got a funny feeling about you creeps, the remainder of your visit will be done in our presence."

Agent #1 walks slowly over to the briefcase and picks it up and while standing only inches from L.T. in a low voice says, "Nigger we are going to see just how committed you are." Both agents depart the room.

Patricia observes L.T.'s questionable facial expression and asks him, "Are you okay?"

L.T. replies, "Yes, I'm fine. Thank you for asking." Approximately two minutes after the agents depart, a helicopter briefly lands on the roof of the building but takes off quickly.

Trying not to upset his staff, L.T. orders everyone back into the conference room to resume their meeting. Nearly two hours later the time is approximately six p.m. L.T. is seated in the backseat of his limousine as he's being driven home by his chauffeur Willie when they notice a crowd gathering around the entrance gate leading into L.T.'s community. Willie slows to a stop by orders of the traffic cop and rolls down his window. As the officer approaches, he

informs them that a bomb blast exploded about thirty minutes ago, but no one was hurt. Suddenly out of nowhere,
Tony Pepco comes running out of the community dressed
in his pajamas shouting, "They've found me. The Mafia
said I wouldn't be able to hide. Those bastards are going
to kill me." A number of the police officers on the scene
take off after Tony. Meanwhile, Willie drives on into the
community to L.T.'s home.

Once inside his elegant home, L.T. is greeted with a
kiss from Olivia who follows him to their bedroom as L.T.
begins to undress and prepare for dinner. As always,
Olivia begins to tell L.T. about her day. She says, "The
children called."

L.T. asks, "What did they say?"

Now sitting on the bed Olivia answers, "Oh Malcolm
called just to say he was thinking of us, and Harriet
phoned to clown around. I tell you that girl should have
been a comedian instead of a lawyer."

L.T. exits from the bathroom and says, "Well when
Malcolm was attending Morehouse you thought that he
was clowning around too much to become a lawyer." L.T.
now prepared for dinner, the two move into the dinning
room.

During dinner Olivia remembers an unclear phone call
she received early and decides to tell L.T. about it. Olivia
says, "There was a rather strange phone call around five
o'clock, but I couldn't quite make it out. The caller didn't
speak very clear, but it sounded like act right, kidnap,
bomb I'm not sure."

A rather concerned look blankets L.T.'s face as he questions, "Do you remember anything at all?"

Olivia, now a little concerned, replies, "No, I can't be
certain of anything he might have said." She then inquires,
"Why is there something wrong?"

L.T. answers, "I'm not sure yet." He then tells Olivia of
the visit by the two men to his office today and about the
explosion at the community's entrance gate.

Olivia asks, "Is that what I heard earlier? Are you sure the men were FBI Agents?"

L.T. replies, "I didn't ask, I hope not but I assume they were." He adds, "But things are sure beginning to look suspicious."

At that moment the phone rings and Olivia answers it. The caller is Thelma who's phoning from a hospital in New Jersey. Having learned of her whereabouts, Olivia informs Thelma that she's putting the phone on speaker so that L.T. may hear the conversation. With her voice cracking as if though she's going to cry any minute Thelma says, "Toby has been admitted and he's unconscious." She adds, "The admissions clerk says an unidentified woman checked him in and left without providing any information. They found our telephone number by searching his wallet for additional information."

L.T. asks, "Mama have the doctors been able to make any kind of a diagnosis?"

Thelma answers, "No, and there is no sign of injury. He's just unconscious." Thelma adds, "But L.T. honey, your daddy and I need to see you at least for a day. Besides, Albert says he has something troubling him that he really needs to talk with you about." L.T. assures her that they'll visit but just for a day. Thelma is relieved to hear the news and hangs up.

Meanwhile at a luxurious hotel ballroom in Sacramento, California there is ballroom dancing and a gala celebration going on. Tuxedos and evening gowns are the attire as Republican David Scott holds a thousand dollar a plate fund raiser. On the stage there is a red, white, and blue banner that reads David's slogan, "Maintain The American Way." There are also long tables and a podium with microphones set up. Seated at the guest of honors table are David, his wife Sara, along with his mother Rachel, and father Philip, and some long time friends. Eric, David's campaign manager, is tonight's host.

Eric is now standing at the podium, slightly facing the Scott's table. He has just finished introducing the people seated at the guest of honor's table. Eric now turning to face the audience says, "And now Bob will be the first person to roast our guest of honor." Eric adds, "I'm often reminded by both him and David that in high school those two were inseparable."

Bob makes his way to the podium where he places his cocktail glass on the podium and says, "Even though we were best friends, there is one thing that David managed to do without my knowledge." Bob now turning to face David asks, "How in the hell did you persuade Tom Meese to let you be senior class president?" David shrugs his shoulders, and the audience fills with laughter as Bob walks back to his seat.

Eric now standing at the podium looking into Bob's direction says, "That's what politics is all about." Then asks, "Does that answer your question?" Laughter again fills the ballroom. Eric turns and faces the audience once again and says, "Speaking of our next speaker I've been told that his vote for whatever reason is usually a big one, I'm talking about Big John Johnson." Once John makes his way to the podium he says, "Eric must be talking about David's first mayoral term, when I was the last person on the Alameda city council to take his money...oh, oh I mean swing my vote." Again laughter fills the ballroom.

Eric once again at the podium looks into John's direction and says, "When the polls close and the votes are counted the majority wins, right?" Eric then announces the next speaker saying, "We'll now hear from the state's previous governor Mr. Jim Robertson."

At the podium Jim speaks saying, "You know, most people who don't know me would probably ask why am I attending a function held in honor of the man who won my office?" Jim adds, "Well my answer is simple—its not whether you win or lose but how you play the game that counts, and I like the way my old opponent plays the political game."

In the midst of applause Eric makes his way back to the podium. Under his breath says, "Very interesting." Eric then says, "Sticking with tradition, we'll now hear from the mother of this campaign Mrs. Rachel."

Mrs. Rachel, who's a spicy eighty-year-old lady, is helped to the podium by David who returns to his seat. First of all Mrs. Rachel looks over at the waiter assigned to her table and demands, "Give me my glass, waiter." She grabs the glass and with a quick glance notices that its empty. Mrs. Rachel inquires, "What good is an empty glass? Hell, put some scotch in it." After the waiter pours her some scotch, Mrs. Rachel, who's now facing the audience says, "As always, I'm glad to see such a good show of support for my boy." She then signals for Eric to adjust the microphone. Mrs. Rachel continues saying, "I don't have any grandchildren so it's not like I have anymore chances after my son in order to get an opportunity to live in the White House."

Mrs. Rachel takes a sip of scotch then comments, "Shit that burns!" She continues saying, "In my wildest imagination, I can see no man, black or otherwise, taking what is rightfully my boy's so tonight I assure you that he is the next president of this country," and points to David. As the audience applauds Mrs. Rachel looks at David says, "Come on. Get up here boy." She then starts to her seat as David makes his way to the podium.

Once at the podium, David raises his hands for quiet and then speaks, "Thanks to each and every one of you for your support—let's maintain the American way." The sound of applause again fills the ballroom. David speaks saying, "It will be an honor to serve as your next president."

"We want Scott. We want Scott," is chanted throughout the ballroom. David signals for his wife Sara to join him at the podium as the chanting continues.

12 CONSEQUENCES DUE TO SOCIETY'S ILLS

The term "perception" alone adequately describes the predicament in which black Americans find themselves, a predicament whereby only a divine power can prevail. The "perception" by America's governing body of its largest group of minorities often results in blacks being labeled as both the "dilemma and the solution" in regards to the discredibility of the nation's global status. Over two hundred years of contributions in numerous areas from American-born blacks have vanished from the consciousness of the nation's policymakers. Such a statement has merit because American-born blacks comprise only twelve percent of the total population yet they make up a whopping ninety percent of the total number of incarcerated personnel.

178

"Perception" has many synonyms. Therefore when synonymizing the word "perception" the synonymist is provided with numerous symbolic substitutes. He will learn that such terms as discernment, awareness, recognition, consciousness, discrimination, judgement, and understanding are all adequate substitutes for the word "perception." Due in part to its many suitable definitions "perception" is therefore capable of providing a steam engine effect regarding one's reality or perhaps derail all of an individual's life long dreams.

Needless to say, for the citizens of America the term "perception" has served as an appalling motive that has served as the match which has ignited numerous societal confrontations. In doing so, "perception," along with both its many disguises and definitions, has managed to thrust the various citizen groups of America into a conflict whereby members from all sides often yield to the impulses of the moment.

"Perception" and "reality" share a strange kinship in that neither is always as it seems. In numerous instances throughout the world, smoke screens and props are used by many as cosmetic fronts. A closer examination of two suitable substitutes for "perception" by blacks could possibly be interpreted: first, "discrimination" might have been practiced in 1781 when nearly four million Americans made up the nation's population and among them were about 650,000 blacks, mostly enslaved, yet had little but the Declaration of Independence to unite them. Secondly, "awareness" reflects the tug-of-war that exists between the interpretations of the Constitution and the Bill of Rights. Therefore, "awareness" can perhaps be summed up as a fiasco that indicates deep-seated problems that have no easy remedies.

Stated simply regardless of the perceived or actual "perception" of African-Americans by their fellow Americans, one facet of reality is certain: if America's present governing body is ever to give due respect to the nation's forefathers for their tremendous accomplishment, that accomplishment being the prodigious task of creating the world's masterpiece of all documents the U.S. Constitution, then the forefather's offspring must first realize something that the previous brain-trust did not— America's black citizens are more than a national problem, they are a part of America. Without a doubt, there is a sad drama being acted out within this stage of life on America's soil between Americans.

While on board their chartered flight to New York, L.T. and Olivia are joined by a few FBI agents along with a couple of staff members. The phone rings. Olivia answers. It's Patricia. As soon as she's done identifying herself, Olivia switches on the speaker phone. In a rather sorrowful voice Patricia says, "We just got news that Ralph and Linda (two staff members) are dead." She adds, "They were discovered early this morning. It is being reported that Ralph died from a heart attack and Linda committed suicide."

A sad stare is frozen upon L.T.'s face as he softly says, "Keep me posted on any more news...especially the autopsy report." He pressed the intercom.

In a soft concerned voice Olivia says, "Someone is trying us. Well, I've got news for them—when the going gets tough, the tough gets going." Mayor Thompson doesn't give a response; he simply turns and looks out the window.

Nearly thirty minutes later, their plane is preparing to land at Kennedy airport. A crowd of reporters and on-lookers are gathered at the terminal. The Thompsons are scheduled to enter. Meanwhile Carlton Davis, who's a fif-teen-year-old dark-skinned brown boy, is among the gath-ered crowd. Carlton lives in L.T.'s old neighborhood in Harlem and he has chosen Democrat Thompson as his role model mainly because Carlton's father was never much of a role model before he got shot during a drug buy gone bad, and his mother is a recovering addict. As L.T. and

Olivia enter the terminal, it's media mania as reporters from both television and newspapers push for a story.

Carlton, along with others, is trying to push himself close enough to at least get a glimpse and hopefully an autograph. Wow! Mayor Thompson and his wife just passed within inches of Carlton who is in his last ditch attempt to get L.T.'s autograph. Carlton simply lowers his head and mows through the crowd following the couple outside. Carlton becomes speechless as L.T. grabs the boy's notebook. L.T. asks, "What is your name young fella?"

A numb Carlton answers, "Carlton sir."

L.T. signs the cover of Carlton's notebook, "To Carlton, a friend always from Democrat Thompson" then hands it to the spellbound Carlton. Afterwards L.T. and Olivia get into a waiting limousine and are driven off to his parents' home. Today Carlton feels like he's on top of the world because the one man he idealizes has signed an autograph for him. A jubilant Carlton tucks his notebook under his jacket so that he might keep it long enough to show his mother and friends at school. Carlton then takes off running for home.

Once at his parents' home, L.T. and Olivia are seated in the living room with Albert discussing Toby's condition when suddenly Thelma enters crying. Albert sits up from his recliner and with a concerned look upon his face asks, "What's the matter honey?"

A teary eyed Thelma answers, "I just talked to Toby and he's fine. He says someone must have put something in his drink. Anyway he's being released tomorrow."

Olivia now moving to comfort Thelma says, "That's wonderful mother."

While looking at L.T. a bewildered Albert says, "Son it's unexplainable changes like that one is the reason I need to talk with you."

In his effort to accommodate his father, L.T. then gets up and grabs a hold of Albert's left hand and leads him out back onto the patio. They sit on the couch, at which time L.T. says, "Let's talk."

Albert rings his hands as he speaks, "Son I've been seeing that scene with the flying dove an awful lot lately."

A perplexed L.T. asks, "Is it some kind of a nightmare?"

Albert appears to be somewhat apprehensive as he answers, "I first saw that scene at the hospital the night your mother gave birth to Toby."

L.T. states, "Daddy that was over 40 years ago."

Albert in a thundering voice says, "It sends chills throughout my body." He takes a deep breath, then adds, "At the most troubling times in my life...I see this dove. This dove— it has an olive twig between its beak as it appears to fly over an apparent burning bush."

A puzzled look blankets L.T.'s face as he tries to speak asking, "I...is there something I can do?"

Albert replies, "No...just whenever I see that dove...nothing...nothing it doesn't matter."

A concerned L.T. urges Albert to continue saying, "Go on daddy, say it."

Albert's face has a wide eyes look, and his hands are in the praying position as he says, "It seems as if though ...shortly after seeing it...a guardian angel removes all my worries from my mind." Albert adds, "But I get an eerie feeling that one of these times my guardian angel's magic isn't going to work."

Both men then pause for a moment before a philosophical Albert inquires, "Son did you know that it is believed that magic is based on misdirection? The culture of a magician's craft is somewhat strange because of the extent that magicians go in order to hide their secrets. Even David Copperfield goes to extra lengths to protect the secrets of his illusions." Albert continues adding, "Perhaps its reasons along those lines that America's minority citizens must continuously be in the mindset of an audience in attendance at a magical show. I mean they must be prepared to suspend their disbeliefs because their reality changes without notice, similar to someone in a performing magician's presence." That statement breaks the same tranquil look L.T. had upon his face that night Albert informed L.T. of the men he's named after. Albert's enlightened words again provide his son with both the ammunition and motivation to meet the challenge that lies ahead.

Upon his and Olivia's return to Clermont, L.T. is pleased to hear that the autopsy performed on Ralph and Linda proves that the couple's deaths were as reported. Meanwhile on the political front, the candidates have been provided with some of the questions that will be asked during the debate. Two days remain before the debate is to take place. Therefore, Mayor Thompson increases his intensity as he studies select areas pertaining to the economy, health care reform, and other national issues including foreign policies. Billy and L.T. discuss government policies and standard operating procedures as they pertain to various topics. Democratic candidate Thompson's preparation is given a boost when he chats with old friends Illinois's Governor Frank Taylor and Michigan's Governor Henry Reed.

This morning, the 28th of September, the day before the debate, L.T. and Olivia board their chartered flight for the nation's capital in the midst of mass media attention at the Orlando airport. Upon the Thompson's arrival at Baltimore Washington International airport, they are greeted by far more media than what they left behind in Orlando. Nonetheless in spite of all the hoopla, the Thompsons enter the waiting limousine without comment. They are driven directly to their hotel where Mayor Thompson and a few staff members review some material before everyone in the party goes sightseeing around town. Meanwhile, Republican Governor David Scott is also greeted by huge media coverage and he too goes straight to his hotel where along with staff members reviews some material that is subject to be debated before sightseeing about town.

This Friday's date, the 29th day of September the year 2008, will forever stand out in America's history because for the first time ever, the offspring of a slave will participate in a one-on-one presidential debate. There are only thirty-four days remaining before voters go to the polls. Therefore, one damaging response by either candidate is certain to cost him votes. The headline of the nation's leading newspaper *America Today* reads, "HOPE CUTS ACROSS EVERY SECTOR IN SOCIETY." That statement sums up the frame of mind of the nation's voters. Throughout the day, television, radio, and newspapers across the country are filled with information pertaining to tonight's debate. Hour after hour as the clock moves towards the eight p.m. eastern time zone start, citizens in restaurants, banks, offices and busy streets are buzzing with discussion of the upcoming debate.

The time now is approximately seven p.m. and as expected, the media has overrun the Ford Theater in an attempt to hear every sound uttered by the candidates as well as catch every twitch they make. It is now 8:10 p.m. and the candidates have been introduced to the general public as well as the panel of seven political analysts. The debate will begin by having each candidate state his campaign slogan and what message into which that slogan translates for the nation's voters. Republican David Scott will be the first candidate to speak. He states, "My presidential slogan states, 'Maintain The American Way.'" David continues adding, "Its message to America's voters provides them with a guarantee that a committed staff will pursue the relentless quest for global excellence in the same trailblazing manner that previous presidents have."

Democrat Luther Thompson states, "My slogan states, 'Shattering The Myths' and its message is to appeal to the conscious of this nation's entire population for moral assistance." L.T. continues adding, "Once translated," he holds up a poster which reads, "Souls Healed Are Tools To Educate, Restrengthen, Igniting Nonstop Gains. Through Holy Enlightenment, Me, You Together Healing Scars." Now after having read the poster to the seven analysts L.T. adds, "Ideologies of this sort are shattering myths this very moment."

Afterwards political analyst Connie Simpson then begins to scan the preprinted questions that each of the candidates are provided and informs the candidates that such questions will be asked within the allotted time frame. Connie then asks, "What legitimate gains can the country expect from your election to office?" She then states, "Democrat Thompson, please respond first."

L.T. replies saying, "My staff and I will do our uttermost to provide the citizens of this nation any legitimate rights he or she may be authorized." He continues saying, "Now the meaning of legitimate as I speak of it means that all citizens will be looked upon as Liberal Elements Going Into The Ideologies Moving America Towards Emancipation, hopefully producing a morally unified nation thereby resulting in an undaunted system by which the government would function."

Republican David Scott then responds stating, "When I am elected to office, the citizens of this nation can expect calculated and realistic methods to resolve any domestic and/or foreign problems encountered."

Analyst Peter Jenson then asked the candidates, "Explain how you and your cabinet members will handle the required cutbacks Congress has projected must be made?" He then states, "Republican Scott, please respond first."

David states, "My staff and I have already devised a plan to stimulate the nation's economy that will offset many of the cutbacks recommended by Congress. This stimulus package includes employment for the disadvantage citizens as well as tax breaks for the prudent citizens."

L.T. then responds saying, "When elected, my staff and I will apply this ideology to the topic of cutbacks, from the letters used to spell cutbacks we will generate, at a minimum, this solution." L.T. continues saying, "After Crediting the Underprivileged Their Bona Fide Accomplishments Currently Kept Secrets, the needed adjustments will be indicted and thoroughly monitored." L.T. concludes saying, "Afterwards the per capita income of all citizens will be paid according to the fruits of their labor."

Upon L.T.'s completion Debra Bronson asks the candidates, "Describe your party's attitudes at this point within the campaign." She then directs Democrat Thompson to respond first.

L.T. responded by saying, "I'd like to go on record as saying that at this point and time within the campaign the Democratic Party's attitude can best be described with this statement—we the Democrats feel confident that we possess All The Total Ingredients To Undermine Destructive Ethnic Stigmas."

Afterwards David Scott chuckles and says, "The Republican Party doesn't have any fancy saying for describing our attitudes, but I can assure the American voters, ours will always be positive no matter what problems we are faced with."

Barbara Winslow then asks the candidates, "Briefly tell the viewers your personal definition of the term attitude." She then directs Republican Scott, "Please respond first."

David states, "My definition of the term attitude is the state of mind a person has as he copes with the many facets of life daily."

Democrat Thompson then responds saying, "My definition of the term attitude can be described fully by this phrase—your attitude is what describes you, what you want to be, it just may not be what the people see."

Immediately following L.T.'s response, the host announcer thanks each candidate for attending and then informs the audience and television viewers that the coverage time set aside for the debate has expired and local networks will resume broadcasting regularly scheduled programs. Once off the air, television, radio, and newspaper reporters literally swamp the two candidates with a flurry of questions. One of the most important questions asked of the candidates was, "Mr. Candidate, do you think this debate helped your campaign?"

Naturally each man answered, "Yes."

A reporter from the television station "A2Z" then informed L.T. saying, "Candidate Thompson, our early suggestion poll indicates that your performance tonight helped you a great deal. Quite frankly it may have even put you a few percentage points ahead of your opponent." The reporter then asks L.T., "Do you personally feel that you can win this election regardless of what tomorrow's poll may show?"

L.T. replies confidently, "After having emerged from a Harlem ghetto to where I am today, life taught me a long time ago that the answer 'yes I can,' doesn't apply to just some Americans, but to all Americans." L.T. concludes by saying, "Yes I personally feel that my party and I can win this election."

At that very moment L.T.'s press secretary Delores who had fought through the crowd began halting any further comments in the usual manner by yelling, "No comment, no further questions please." L.T. is then able to get into his limousine where Olivia is waiting. They then depart Ford's theater.

Now if there was any question as to how effective L.T.'s performance was during the presidential debate those questions were answered within *America Today* newspaper headline that read, "DEBATE HAS TOSSED BRICK EFFECT, AS IT SHATTERS MYTHS." Perhaps the nation's voters weren't totally familiar with Candidate Thompson prior to the debate but they sure are now. This morning at breakfast tables across the country, the topic of conversation is that of the debate's outcome. Radio disc

188 ◆ SHATTERING THE MYTHS

jockeys are declaring Democrat Thompson the winner. So too are their listeners.

The media's Gallup polls are reflecting the enormous ground that Democrat Thompson has gained, nearly fifteen percentage points since the start of the presidential campaign. If the election was held today, the poll results show that Republican Scott would get 50% of the votes, while Democrat Thompson would receive 43% of the votes and 7% of the voters are undecided, considering the polls margin of error of plus or minus five percent. A few polls are suggesting that Thompson might be leading the campaign. Nonetheless political analysts and the media agree that this election should be referred to as "America's Ultimate Presidential Election."

With less than five weeks remaining before election day, the media reports that it's up to the candidates themselves to win or lose the upcoming election. At this particular juncture in the election, now more than ever, each candidate's comments, actions and even leisure time activities are being watched very closely. Therefore, topics like voter turnout and absentee voting are of major concerns.

However, the nation's predicted weather conditions are generating slight concerns, as blizzard conditions unlike any before are expected for the New England states as early as tomorrow. And the National Weather Forecasters are predicting the conditions could last for the remainder of the year. But the most frightening predictions are not those forecasts—they are the ones regarding the southeastern part of the country. The weather forecasters are predicting that due to a unique frontal system, torrential rain mixed with ice will hit a stretch of eight mostly southern states. The change in weather is expected approximately one week before election day, and could last nearly eight weeks. Those targeted states are Maryland, Virginia, North Carolina, South Carolina, Georgia, Alabama, Mississippi, and Louisiana.

The unpredictable weather isn't the only topic that is in question. Besides at this point the weather predictions aren't a major concern, with an election of this magnitude and the candidates running neck and neck. Meanwhile, at their headquarters, each candidate, along with their family and staff members, is weighing major concerns. Republican candidate David Scott's major concerns are due in part to the possibility of Democrat Thompson's friendship with the governors of Illinois and Michigan, which could result in his loss of those powerful states. Another concern that looms large over the Republican's camp pertains to Thompson's chances of carrying his present home state of Florida as well as his birth state of New York. Now if both cases were to happen, Scott would lose those four states total of 98 electoral votes which represent over one-third of the required electoral votes needed in order to win the election.

Meanwhile, a big hurdle looms on the Democratic front as well—the big misconception held by the black southern voters regarding Democrat Thompson's identity with his blackness. The majority of those black voters reside in the eight aforementioned states which have been predicted to encounter uniquely harsh winter conditions around the time frame of the election, again highlighting the topics of voter turnout and absentee ballots. As a result of these obstacles, both candidates focus on the armed forces personnel in a last ditch effort to win votes.

In addition to courting the men and women in uniform as well as U.S. citizens abroad, the candidates and their supporters are spearheading massive voter registration drives. The Democrats have spent a whopping seven million dollars on voter registration, and transportation to and from the polls. Democratic supporters are also educating many voters about the importance of electoral votes and the overall election process. Both party's feel so strongly about the importance of the early and absentee voting that they have set up separate committees to oversee those areas.

The record shows that the disgruntled registered voters aren't questioning the fact that L.T.'s skin is black; what they are referring to is how will blacks benefit from Democrat Thompson's election to the oval office. The reason that sparked the voters to look upon candidate Thompson in this light is due in part to some information that has become known to the general public. These findings aren't degrading or anything like that; however, they are not the common characteristics of a black man either. It must be noted that these voters have learned of some comments spoken by the Mayor during an interview with "News Hour Magazine." During that interview, L.T. confessed that from early childhood, throughout college and even today, he's not athletically inclined in regards to playing basketball, football, nor baseball. However, if anyone challenged him to a tennis match or a round of golf, or even bowling then he'd take on all challengers.

During that interview Democrat Thompson also admitted, "I have listened to rap music enough to know that a large amount of the music doesn't represent my viewpoints in the references often made regarding black women and women in general, including the terms used when referring to another black man or references made regarding killing police officers. Therefore, the music has a small place in my life because only a small percentage of it carries the true message of blacks and their right to vent themselves."

On the other hand Democrat Thompson stated that, "Reggae music and it's lyrics did play a role in molding some of my ideas while growing up."

During the interview in question L.T. was asked, "How in the world could you have been born and raised in a Harlem ghetto and not have any of the community's activities effect you?"

Democrat Thompson replied, "Because none of the role models that I was trying to emulate lived there."

This remark prompted the interviewer to ask, "Who were the role models that you were trying to emulate?"

The Mayor replied, "The three men whom I am named after—my great-great-grandfather, Mr. Booker T. Washington, and Dr. Martin Luther King Jr."

After reports from the interview were made public, the polls showed a slight decline across southern states regarding Democrat Thompson's rating that has resulted in mixed reports due in part to the margin of error that consists in all polls. However on the homefront, Democrat Thompson's campaign staff members have informed him that at the present time, the big picture projects that he could lose all eight of those states.

Today is the 25th of October the year 2008. It is now ten days before the election date of 4 November. Weather in the New England states is following the forecasters' predictions. Blizzard conditions unlike any the state's citizens have ever witnessed are blanketing the hillsides, with no letup in sight. If the predictions of the southern and southeastern states materialize, this election's weather conditions will also be recorded in America's history right up there with the outcome.

This Tuesday marks exactly one week before election day and just as the forecasters predicted, icy rain has begun to fall across the eight aforementioned states. Nonetheless the U.S.A. braces itself for what has been labeled the country's ultimate presidential election. Equally important are the absentee vote results which shows California's Governor Scott holding a commanding lead in all four regions of the country. Those results reflect only about three percent of the nation's voters. But in the minds of both candidates, absentee votes as well as voter registration prove to be topics that in no way can be taken lightly. Therefore both men will attend one last voter rally in the city of Trenton, New Jersey on Monday.

Meanwhile political analysts are discussing the possibility of holding the New England states election on Saturday the 1st of November mainly because this coming weekend has been predicted as the last possible few days for a month that the citizens might be able to travel any place at all. Therefore the candidates are informed of this change and the matter later becomes official after both the House and the Senate voted "yes." This Saturday, the 1st of November, is election day for the states of Maine, Vermont, New Hampshire, Massachusetts, Rhode Island, and Connecticut.

With the passing of each tick of the clock, it's becoming more evident that this election's outcome will be etched into America's history. Meanwhile, the staff at both candidates headquarters are calculating a series of moves, now that the simmering smoke of this election might turn into a blazing fire at any moment in light of how quickly things can change. Again it appears that there is no letup in sight regarding the inclement weather that's hammering down on several southeastern states.

Today throughout the New England states, most of the roadways have been cleared enough for the voters to get to and from the polls. Meanwhile, the candidates are at home with family and staff members glued to their television sets. David Scott is supported by his wife and parents along with a few staff members; so too are L.T. and Olivia. The candidates are concerned with today's results because there are a total of 37 electoral votes at stake, as well as the identification of the true early leader before the rest of the nation's polls open on super Tuesday.

The first results aren't broadcast until noon eastern time due to the checking of both the machines and the handwritten ballot counts. They both must be the same in the event that the heavy snow knocks out the power lines before the polls close. The first reports shows that Democrat Thompson has a surprisingly large lead in all the states except Connecticut, where he is losing badly. These results reflect approximately fifty percent of the votes counted, but the polls do not close for another six hours. As expected, the mood of each party's headquarters depends upon if you're Democrat or Republican. Both candidates spend their day pacing the floor, stopping only at the sight and sound of updates. It's now 7 p.m. eastern standard time and the polls have been closed in all the New England states for over an hour.

BEEP! BEEP! BEEP! All the major television networks coverage of the election are prepared to announce the early election results and identify the leader. Gail Anderson the anchorwoman for the television station "A2Z" from Washington D.C. broadcast begins like this, "Congratulations, Democrat Thompson, as you've been declared the winner in five of the New England states, losing only Connecticut." Everyone at L.T.'s Clermont headquarters jumps with joy over the news as the phone begin to ring and congratulations begin to pour in from across the country. But L.T. is quick to caution everyone who phones that it's still early yet. A look at the electoral votes show that by virtue of tonight's five state victory, has a total of twenty-nine electoral votes while Republican Scott, on the heels of his Connecticut victory has only eight.

Meanwhile in Trenton, N.J., preparation is underway at the voters rally sites of both the Democrats and Republicans parties. A glimpse at the dark side of this campaign reveals two men plotting an assassination attempt. At this very minute, a helicopter pilot and the FBI's top assassin are in the lone abandoned building directly across the street from the Democrats' rally site. A brief description of the rally site shows that the convention center has a canopy covering the entrance. Surrounded by wooden props in a secluded corner of the abandoned building, the assassin skillfully scans the surroundings of both the convention center and those of the abandoned building. Having carefully studied the surroundings, the assassin confidently turns to the pilot and says, "It will take him approximately ninety seconds to walk from his car to underneath the canopy. I'll nail him during that time."

The pilot asks, "Are you sure that you can draw an accurate site on a moving target in such a short period of time?"

The assassin replies as he points to a gun case that holds a 30.0.6 rifle with a scope, "With my trusty baby here, in a minute and a half, at five hundred meters, I can hit the crown of an unborn baby's head."

The frightened pilot asks, "Would you?"

The assassin replies, "For the past ten years, I've lived abroad in Europe, Italy, and Sweden, going about as I please and even though I've not stepped foot into the U.S. until today, I'm still the FBI's number one political assassin. I have been hired to spend approximately three hours inside the States with return reservations via chartered plane to Frankfurt." The assassin adds, "For seven million, there isn't anyone I wouldn't kill." He then takes this moment to enlighten the pilot saying, "I've only been shot once in my life but it was several times, back in the seventh grade. Since that time I've carried out exactly thirty-four jobs for exactly thirty-four million dollars. I've never failed nor have I ever taken a job for less than one million dollars. However, this one is worth seven million. I'm going to take care of that candidate. The assassin concludes by saying, "Now you know why I top the FBI's list of assassins."

On the other side of the city at the airport, an unsuspecting Mayor Thompson exits his chartered plane accompanied by his lovely wife, parents and the elder Robinsons, and a few staff members and a host of security guards. Candidate Thompson briefly works the crowd of supporters, shaking hands and signing autographs before entering his limousine. Shortly after arriving at the hotel Olivia unpacks and prepares L.T.'s outfit to be worn at this evening's rally. Lastly, she places his gray hat on a chair next to the bed.

Due to Susanna's bad bout with the flu, she and Walter will not attend the rally. Neither will the elder Thompson's who have decided to stay with the Robinsons. As Olivia and L.T. are getting dressed to attend the rally, their parents are in the suite talking of the good old days as they enjoy television. Suddenly Thelma gets a motherly intuition; she feels all is not okay, but she can't seem to put her finger on it at the moment. The time now is 5:30 p.m. and Olivia and L.T., along with the others in their entourage, leave the hotel en route to the rally site.

Shortly after L.T.'s departure, Thelma discovers the gray hat he intended to wear lying on a chair. She picks it and up pulls it to her breast and begins to weep uncontrollably. Albert and Susanna hear Thelma's weeping and enter the room to confront her at which time she looks to them and says, "My baby didn't wear his hat because today he needs to be seen clearly."

In spite of the inclement weather forecast for Trenton and the surrounding areas, the rain has stopped at the moment, yet it is cold but unusually clear for such late hour in the day. Furthermore at a well-secluded site within an abandoned high-rise building overlooking the entrance to the convention center is the nation's most notorious assassin. The first sign of Candidate Thompson's arrival is the appearance of two sedans filled with security people who take up their positions. Spies for the assassin along the route of Mayor Thompson's motorcade have radioed word to the assassin that his target is approximately seven minutes away.

The cool professional unzips the gun case exposing the three parts of his rifle along with a box of bullets. Then a black gloved hand grabs hold of the barrel while the other black gloved hand grabs the rifle butt. He carefully connects the two parts. A black gloved hand then grabs a hold of the scope lens and carefully the gunman attaches it onto the powerful weapon. Methodically the assassin goes through his normal routine. Then he loads three rounds into the rifle, ejecting one into the chamber where it's ready to be fired by just the slightest touch of the trigger. He then raises the rifle up to his face and places it into his left shoulder where he looks into the scope lens. He then moves the rifle slowly about the gathered crowd below, carefully adjusting the scope's sight until the picture is crystal clear.

Nearly one minute after the gunman has prepared himself L.T.'s navy blue limousine rolls to a stop among the crowd. Patricia is first to exit the car, followed by Olivia and L.T. as they begin walking among security to the entrance way. True to his word, the assassin quickly gets L.T. into his scope sight and with his hand on the trigger, he adjusts the sight picture so that he is actually able to count the gray hairs about L.T.'s head. BUT! HE LOWERS HIS WEAPON, THEN HE QUICKLY RAISES IT AGAIN AND WITH HIS HAND ON THE TRIGGER FINE TUNES THE SCOPE EVEN MORE! AT THIS TIME THE ASSASSIN IS ABLE TO SEE THE PLACE WHERE L.T. NICKED HIMSELF SHAVING. "THAT'S L.T.— HE SAVED MY LIFE, I WON'T DO THIS!" Geno then breaks down his rifle as L.T. walks under the canopy leading to the entrance. Geno quickly runs out to the waiting helicopter and orders the pilot to take him to the hideout and without question the pilot obeys. Meanwhile in the helicopter, Geno and the pilot don't speak a word until they arrive at the hideout and Geno signals for the pilot to land.

Geno then rushes inside where he meets face to face with the mastermind behind the entire scheme, Mrs. Rachel Scott who says, "Good you're here." She holds up a briefcase and says, "Your money is in here." Geno has his Uzi machine gun at his side.

As he pauses he observes the two men who lied as being FBI agents standing beside Mrs. Rachel, who ask, "What the Sam hell are you doing?"

Mrs. Rachel, now clearly disturbed says, "I'm prepared to pay you seven million dollars cash! Did you kill that black bastard?" Mrs. Rachel asks.

Geno then walks over to Mrs. Rachel and stares her straight into her eyes and says, "If anyone harms any member of the Thompson family I will personally kill you and your entire family."

A stunned Mrs. Rachel grabs a hold of her chest because she can't believe what is happening. Geno then returns to the helicopter and orders the pilot to take him to a remote air strip so that he can link up with his flight crew. Without hesitation the pilot obeys.

Meanwhile at the convention center, Democrat Thompson mingles with well over three thousand new voters before the rally ends. Afterwards the Mayor and his wife leave his well-wishers and return to the hotel where a relieved Thelma breaks down in tears as she hugs her son. Before long everyone is calm as they bed down for the night. The media reports that both presidential candidates had a fine turnout last night at their respective voter drives. Both men leave the city early the following morning en route back to their headquarters in preparation for the election.

As both Olivia and L.T. awake, this morning brings with it a sense of newness for life and everything associated with living. Today, the 4th of November the year 2008, is very special to the Thompsons not because its election day but because it assures the both of them that they aren't dreaming; the Thompsons are standing squarely on the threshold of history. It isn't long before L.T. and Olivia are dressed and seated at the breakfast table with the family and staff discussing the possibilities of today's election. Billy Tubbs, along with his family, is in Austin, Texas. He and his family, along with some campaign staff members, will fly to Clermont once they have voted.

For decades the first Tuesday in the month of November every four years has been known as Election Day throughout America. The results of this election usually send rippling effects across the entire face of the globe. The victor's name of this election is immediately known from Berlin, Germany to Moscow and every nation in between. Within the United States trading and stocks on Wall Street are subject to imitate the movement of a single sheet of paper caught in the midst of a hurricane. The history and tradition associated with the oval office of the USA can't ever be justifiably defined by any one person, be he an elected official or otherwise. However this presidential election will be like none other in the history of this great nation.

Since a lackluster showing during the debate by Republican David Scott has resulted not only in the introduction of Democrat Luther Thompson to the American voters but also Thompson's charisma has generated what many voters are referring to as spooky possibilities. Perhaps this election's outcome is summed up best by the numerous newspapers across the nation who's headlines read the same as America Today which simply reads "IF."

Republican David Scott and family along with a few of his staff members are at his Sacramento, California home. David's vice-presidential choice, New York's Governor George Conners, and family will fly out to California after they vote. The time is now nine a.m. eastern time and the polls are open across the country except for the states of Maryland, Virginia, North Carolina, South Carolina, Georgia, Alabama, Mississippi, and Louisiana. Due to a cold freeze that swept across those states overnight, power has been knocked out and many power lines are encased in ice. Therefore the polls within those states won't open before two p.m. eastern time and will close at two a.m. eastern time, seven hours after the west coast polls will have closed.

Both candidates and their running mates have voted and at this very minute both vice-presidential candidates are en route to join their running mate. It's now noon eastern time and nine a.m. Pacific, as early returns show the candidates virtually tied in almost every state, with approximately 20% of the votes counted; in New York Republican Scott has 11% and Democrat Thompson has 9%. In Pennsylvania with 22% of the votes counted Democrat Thompson has 12% and Republican Scott has 10%. Now a look at how the candidates are doing in their home states reports shows that in Florida, Democrat Thompson leads Republican Scott by a whopping margin of 25% as the election board shows, with 27% of Florida's votes counted. However in Republican Scott's home state, the lead is reversed as Scott leads by 16% with 20% of the votes counted.

Throughout the day Americans have been glued to their television sets and radios as the nation's ultimate presidential election unfolds. The networks returns have the resemblance of a boxing match between two undefeated champions who are heading into the final round, as they continue to score alternating victories. The time is now eight p.m. eastern time and five p.m. Pacific as the television station "A2Z" anchorwoman Gail Anderson, along with political analyst Tom Meese, report and explain the election returns with the use of a replica board of the United States.

They report begins with the candidates home states, starting in Florida where Democrat Thompson with 89% of the vote has been projected the winner with 97% of the votes counted. In California, Republican Scott with 89% of the vote has been declared the winner with 95% of the votes counted. Democrat Thompson has also picked up huge victories in the states of New York with 57% of the votes as well as receiving 59% in Illinois and 59% in Michigan.

Republican Scott is also doing his part at keeping this election a toss-up; he has been projected the winner in several states that have double digit electoral votes. Republican Scott has won Ohio with 55% and Pennsylvania with 57% of the total votes. Now add New Jersey to

Scott's list of states where he has been projected the winner with 53% of the total vote count. As more and more results become public, the candidates seem to split them as this election lives up to its billing and is shaping up in a manner where those eight frozen states might decide the outcome. A look at the political analyst's big board shows the highlighted states are critical because they have double digit electoral votes.

The total number of electoral votes are 538 and in order to be declared the election's winner, a candidate must receive at least 270 electoral votes. Which means a candidate can receive as many as 268 electoral votes and yet lose the election. Therefore Tom Meese is standing before the big replica explaining this process to the television viewers. Tom also informs the viewers that, "There are twenty states with ten or more electoral votes. Of those twenty states, fifteen have already been decided." Tom adds, "Republican Scott has won eight and Democrat Thompson has won seven of those states, and five remain, due to the unique weather conditions previously mentioned regarding the south and southeastern states."

The time is now 10:30 p.m. eastern standard time and all the polls are closed except for those in the eight affected states where the early reports show Republican Scott leading in all the states by an average margin of three percentage points. So far, the voter turnout is light and many voters are just getting off from work but the road conditions are improving as the traffic picks up. At this point only about thirty percent of the votes are counted. Meanwhile a look at the candidates' totals to this point show that Democrat Thompson is leading with a total of 244 electoral votes while Republican Scott trails with a total of 213 votes.

These totals mean that from the eight remaining states there are a total of 83 electoral votes, five of those states which are Maryland, Virginia, North Carolina, Georgia, and Louisiana have at least ten electoral votes at stake. Now a look at what Republican Scott must have happen in order for him to win is this: first of all Scott must pick up at least 57 more electoral votes which would give him a total of 270 the minimum needed to win. Secondly, in order for Republican Scott to pick up those 57 votes, he must win at least five of the remaining states but, if one of those five states doesn't carry ten or more electoral votes then Scott must win six of the remaining states to be declared the winner. On the other hand, Democrat Thompson must first pick up at least 26 more electoral votes for the minimum 270 required to win. Secondly, in order for Democrat Thompson to pickup those 26 votes, he must win at least four of the remaining states, any four states, and Thompson wins the election. However, at this juncture in the election, it should be mentioned that nothing is certain.

As the election's scenario unfolds at the homes of each candidate, each man sits alone and in his mind deep reflections are being recalled. Republican Scott's mind is reflecting back to his twenty percentage points lead prior to the debate. Meanwhile at his home, Democrat Thompson sits alone and as he hears family and friends in the other room react to the updates. At this moment L.T. can't help reflecting back to the meeting at which time his campaign staff informed him that he could possibly lose all of the states that are experiencing the unusual weather.

L.T.'s attention is suddenly interrupted by Olivia's voice as she's calling him to get the telephone saying, "It's Arthur." L.T. is perplexed as to why Arthur Reed would be calling especially at this time on election night.

Arthur introduces himself, then assures L.T. that it is him. Arthur then attempts to inform L.T. about some critical information. But as Arthur begins to explain, the telephone line suddenly begins to static and become unclear on L.T.'s end but Arthur continues talking. Hoping that the line might clear up, L.T. continues to hold the receiver. Even though L.T. cannot hear Arthur, Arthur tries to inform L.T., "Myself and the other nine leaders who asked that you run for the presidency from various organizations and our organizations consist of over 100,000 registered voters in each of the states still up for grabs. We have succeeded in rallying these voters behind you." A bewildered L.T. is still unable to make out what Arthur is saying, when suddenly L.T. hears cheering and shouting in the living room so loud that he has thoughts of hanging up. Instead L.T. decides to allow Arthur a few seconds more.

The time is now 1:55 a.m. and as Thelma and all the others began cheering the results, Albert is unable to move at all! An immobilized Albert once again witnesses the scene of a dove flying over an apparent burning bush! No sooner has a reluctant L.T. hung up the phone than an ecstatic Olivia bursts through the door shouting, "We won! Honey we won!" Olivia is hardly able to catch her breath long enough to tell L.T. that members from both parties are verifying all the counted votes to insure that all the absentee votes are included in the final total. L.T. is swamped by his immediate family and friends but he wants to be certain of the outcome before celebrating. The celebration will have to wait until Patricia and Malcolm, along with Harriet and other staff members who are witnessing the vote count procedures, report the outcome.

It seem as if though since the news, time has become a blur even though the time is now 2:45 a.m. The entire nation is still awake, that is until the final vote tally and Democrat Luther Thompson is declared the WINNER! By the slimiest margin in modern history Democrat Thompson received 53% of the popular vote to 47% for Republican Scott, and (D) Thompson received 277 electoral votes to (R) Scott's 263. Of the last eight states to vote (D) Thompson won four which were South Carolina, Alabama, Mississippi, and Louisiana. All four carry less than ten electoral votes for a total of 33 of the potential 83 votes.

Meanwhile (R) Scott won all four of the states that has ten electoral votes or more they are Maryland, Virginia, North Carolina, and Georgia for a total of 50 of the potential 83 votes. An examination of the election shows that no candidate won either of the last eight states by more than five percent of the votes.

Upon the decision becoming official that Democrat Thompson is declared the winner, pandemonium breaks out in the Thompson's home and headquarters. Democrat Thompson and family are en route to his headquarters to meet and thank his supporters. Meanwhile Republican Scott and family used the reporters who surrounded him to shout for a recount! But their protest is to no avail. Daylight comes quickly in the minds of most who stayed up to witness the election's heartstopping outcome which to many was worth the lost sleep. On this, the 5th of November 2008, a new chapter in American history is written. The nation's newspaper headlines says it best as they read, "IN AMERICA, YOU TOO CAN SHATTER THE MYTHS."

There is a baffling equation that governs this nation. Its components are cultural differences, opportunity, and money which equals the American Dream. A closer examination reveals that status is the common denominator of the components. For numerous black Americans the partitions that separate their dreams from reality are elaborate decoys comprised of the term status. Stated simply, "Status is a thief of dreams."

It is both sad and unfortunate that the winds of change have not blown the sediments of prejudice from America's grass roots. An even greater disturbing perception indicates that the court's attitude mirror that of the country. Such a paradox is evident in the relationship between the nation's two largest groups, black and white Americans. However, the grievances between blacks and whites seem to comprise such an unsettling void that no mortal man nor group of mortal men are likely to fill. Stated simply, the nation's citizens need to witness another (Immaculate Conception) miracle.

There is little doubt that many Americans live in a state of quiet desperation. Because along with the label of U.S. citizen, many Americans shoulder an even greater responsibility—that of contributor. The land of the free and the home of the brave is also the land where, "Affection is the soil that contains the roots of wholesome existence." Within every previously noted instance lies an unseen obstacle called survival. In order to survive in this country, one must have a means to generate money, because money is required in order to convert dreams to reality. Without a doubt this nation's cultural differences exist because of the desire to have a reality that reflects one's dreams.

Today, on this 16th day of January 2009, in the nation's capital the weather is unexplainably clear and a mild sixty degrees as the ceremonial oath of office takes place in the traditional manner. Shortly after having taken the oath of office, President Luther Taliaferro Thompson delivers his Inaugural Address during which he states, "The making of an American begins at the point where he himself rejects all other ties, any other history, and himself adopts the disposition of his adopted land. My fellow Americans, let us unite with one heart and one mind. Let it be clearly understood that every difference of opinion is not a difference in principle. It is without question that we are different in appearance therefore, we are called by different names. Nonetheless, let us become brethren of the same principle.

"Throughout the campaign I was often reminded of an old cliché that reads, 'Simply wanting to accomplish a task is only a fraction of the requirement needed in order to get the job done. Actually achieving the task in question is the way that character is built.' As I stand before you today, I represent what this nation can produce which is a multiethnic society where everyone's dreams can become reality. Therefore I say to each of you today that, 'He who has imagination without learning, has wings but no feet.' I would like to take this opportunity to remind each of you that success begins with a decision; failure to make a decision results in failure to succeed. And even though we all must attempt to clear various hurdles and climb the ladder of life rung by rung in order to achieve our goal. Nonetheless we all are capable of SHATTERING THE MYTHS regarding hurdles that society indicates can not be cleared."

THE END